THE JOYS AND JOLTS OF RETIREMENT

by

Kim Swezey

ISBN: 0-75962-517-4

This book is printed on acid free paper.

1stBooks – rev. 7/27/01

FRONT COVER

The author, six grandchildren and a nephew. Left to right: Nancy Swezey, Kim Swezey, Trish Swezey, Thomas Maust, Liz Carney, Myles Salazar (nephew), Kimmie Swezey, Annie Carney

BACK COVER

Nancy and Kim Swezey

TABLE OF CONTENTS

PREFACE

I have a close and loving family. And I certainly want to keep it that way, so I haven't written extensively about any of them. Nancy, my wife of 50 years, is a warm, caring and supportive friend and companion. We have six children. Our eldest John and Dana have both been married and divorced and, although only one has remarried, they appear to be leading happy and steady lives. Between them, they have five daughters: Trish, Nancy, Kimberly, Elizabeth and Annie — all of whom bring great joy to their parents and to Nancy and me.

Three of our daughters, Karen, Barbara and Patricia, are closely involved in an ashram (meditation center) and are devotees of Gurumayi. The ashram has enhanced their lives and they are wonderful, thoughtful women. Our youngest is Carolyn, happily married to Peter, and together they produced the first boy in our family, Thomas, after ten girls in a row. Thomas is a handsome youngster, and is autistic — but the newest therapies seem to be helping him.

We all get together often and even vacation together several times a year.

For over forty years I worked as a retailer in the family department store started by my grandfather. The 70's and 80's were especially good business years and, although we were putting six kids through college, we were able to invest occasionally and luckily. So, along with the store's retirement plan, Social Security, fortunate investments and some inheritances, we have a comfortable cushion which allows us to have a full and exciting retirement.

To quote Brendan Gill, a "New Yorker" writer who died recently at 83 — "Life is not fair, and I have always been happily aware of this. From the cradle I have been unjustly dealt with, always very much to my advantage."

CHAPTER 1

SEX, DRUGS AND ROCK & ROLL

— Woodstock Remembered —

It was 1969 and I was having dinner with the soon-to-be-fired Superintendent of Schools of nearby Bellport. We were discussing the rebelliousness of high school youth. I had a son who was going through this — anti-establishment, anti-Vietnam, pro-pot and long hair.

My dinner partner said, "It's so important to try and connect — to do something interesting or exciting with the kids of today." I took his idea seriously and mulled it over for a few days.

My son, John, and his friends had been talking about wanting to go to the Woodstock Rock Festival. When I told them I'd take them they jumped for joy. John, 15, my sister's son Bill, 17, and two of their friends excitedly drove with me to the Catskills for what was billed as the biggest rock concert ever. Little did we know.

The Festival actually ended up being in Bethel, sixty miles from Woodstock. Max Yasgur rented part of his 600-acre farm of gently rolling hills and a herd of 650 Guernsey cows. Max was quoted as saying, "If the generation gap is to be closed, we older people have to do more than we have done."

We were fortunate to arrive before the great crush of people — estimated at over 400,000 — descended on Bethel. We parked in a field near a small deli about a mile from the site of the concert.

Soon all the roads within twenty miles of the site were clogged with cars and people. Then came the deluge. Heavy rains and wind turned the Yasgur farm into a muddy sea like wet, grassy chocolate. But it didn't dampen the spirits of the thousands of young people from all over the East Coast. They slid in the mud and bathed in the rain. Most of the young women wore tee shirts and it became quite a wet tee shirt fair. My boys enjoyed picking out the "pointees" and the "roundees."

Soon the weather let up and the Rock Festival was on. The boys went to the first night concert while I stayed and slept in the car. They reported back with great enthusiasm about the night's musicians — Joan Baez, Arlo Guthrie, Richie Havens, Sweetwater, et. al.

My nephew Bill slept under the hospital trailer the first night. He was just out of a hospital after a rather severe car accident. That night the hospital trailer collapsed. He was not hurt but he did stiffen up and had trouble walking the rest of the stay. His mother, my sister, wanted him home after the first night, but

1

there was absolutely no way to drive out of there. We had to stay until the muddy but joyous end.

The next day I went to the Festival site. There was some transportation — small pick up trucks — going back and forth. If you were lucky you could jump on. Everyone was squashed together so that when a young lady was next to me — I vividly remember this — fleshy parts of her body pressed tightly up against me. I found this quite exciting, though the young lady never looked my way.

Arriving at the Festival I was startled by seeing a young man completely naked run past screaming and waving his arms. A "bad acid trip" was the report, and he was soon attended to by the medics there. Forty-five doctors had flown in on helicopters to provide medical aid to the vast throngs. The performers and food were also helicoptered in. Once the Festival began, helicopters were the only way in or out.

There was a large raised stage with towers for the lights and sound system. In front of the stage was huge mass of young people sitting quietly, for the most part, on the rolling farm fields, sprawled on blankets and plastic tarps. I had never seen such an immense gathering. Virtually all were teenagers or in their twenties, and quite a few families, young married (?) couples with small children. One local policeman said, "Notwithstanding their personalities, their dress and their ideas, they were the most courteous, considerate, and well-behaved group of kids I have ever been in contact with in my twenty-four years of police work." tee shirts, jeans, long printed skirts or dresses, beads and unkempt long hair was the look of the day.

A large tent to one side of the stage was reserved for the performers and stage hands. Since I was the only forty-plus-year-old in the audience, I was treated as an "electrician" and had access to the performers' tents. This provided me with fresh fruit, water and a close-up view of rock musicians in repose. In spite of their reputations, they appeared and acted no differently than most other groups preparing to go to work.

I was not a great rock fan but the one group that captured my fancy was Sly and the Family Stone. Sly had a sing-a-long that got a most enthusiastic response. "Throw the peace sign up and sing higher higher." Everyone waved two fingers in the air stretching and chanting "higher, higher," an appropriate gesture for the natural and chemically-induced euphoria of this Rock Festival.

The peace theme and anti-Vietnam sentiment were widely shared by this audience. One performer, John Sebastian, I think, led the responsive throng in:

1, 2, 3, 4
What are we fighting for?
Don't ask me
I don't give a damn
Next stop is Vietnam

2

5, 6, 7, 8
Open up the pearly gates
Skinny dipping is beautiful.

Max Yasgur, the farmer, was introduced on the stage and was warmly greeted when he gave everyone the peace sign. Announcements were made warning about bad brown acid. "If you feel like experimenting only take a half a tablet." Yeah. And there was skinny dipping in the nearby ponds for cleanliness and for showing off — and quite open sexual encounters. I vividly recall during a mild warm rain shower standing under a tent flap and watching couples in the nearby fields. One couple walked hand-in-hand through the damp grass then lay down, undressed, and passionately performed oral sex on each other. They rose, smiled at one another, holding hands again, and walked slowly away in the gentle rain, a new American idyll.

Eating (food that is) was a bit of a problem though no one seemed concerned. Women in the local Jewish Community Center made thousands of sandwiches and they were distributed by the nuns of the Convent of St. Thomas — a most appropriate ecumenical gesture. Near where we parked Hasidic Jews in their felt fedoras, long silk coats, and long curls passed out water and slices of bread. The Hasidics are ultra-Orthodox Jews who come from Brooklyn to spend their summers in the Catskills.

One young lady who was there said, "There were seven of us. We lost everybody. We had no food, no water. People gave it to us. We had hamburgers and ice cream for breakfast. Everybody is so nice to everybody. Everybody is sharing."

During the Festival there was one death (drug overdose), two births and five miscarriages.

Though I was supposedly the chaperon — probably the only one of the 400,000 there — I didn't see a great deal of the boys. I did call home one night. Bill's mother, my sister, was frantic. "Where have you taken my son?" News reports of the Festival had painted it a disaster, one of rain, mud, roads clogged, no food or water. Meanwhile we were all having the time of our lives.

I recently asked John and Bill what their recollections were. John — "It was a huge muddy mess but I remember sitting in about the same spot on the hill for three days listening to the great rock bands: Sly, the Who, Jefferson Airplane, Credence Clearwater, and I especially recall Jimi Hendrix (who later died of a drug overdose) singing 'The Star-Spangled Banner.' Bill — "After the first day I could hardly move my leg. But still it was great! Everyone was sharing their food and pot — though we didn't smoke."

Then I asked the 64 dollar question: Did it make a difference, i.e. in our relationship? Bill — "I've been talking about you taking us there for twenty-

3

eight years." John — "It was a mammoth gesture on your part. I've never forgotten!"

It certainly didn't solve the problems of growing up in the late 60's and early 70's, but we had a great time together and have had a solid relationship ever since.

POSTSCRIPT

In July of 1997, I went to visit three daughters who live near or in an ashram (meditation retreat) in the Catskills. Within ten miles, I discovered, is Bethel the Woodstock site. I drove over and easily found the original Yasgur farm. On one of the hills was erected a khaki tent with "Woodstock Nation" painted on the side. Next to it was a woman playing the bongo drums and a bearded man playing the guitar. A young boy was with them wearing a peace symbol tee shirt. They were gathered around a flaming fire pit that was built within psychedelically colored rocks.

As I drove by I noticed several police cars. When I stopped, one of them came up to me and asked, "Are you alright?" I said, "Sure," with a quizzical look on my face. Before I could ask, "What's up?" he drove on. I saw a car belonging to a local newspaper and a photographer taking pictures. Further down the road two policemen were talking to two men in suits and ties. It turned out the suited men were lawyers for the new owners of the farm (Max Yasgur had died). They wanted the tent down and no one camping there overnight.

The lawyers approached the couple by the fire. After a five-minute conversation — the only words of which I could hear were "Peace, Love, and Democracy" — the two groups shook hands and the bearded man took down the tent.

Then a van of six young people arrived, too young to have been at the original Festival. The bongo-playing woman, whose name I found out was Abigail Storm, proceeded to give them a fifteen minute lecture on the Woodstock Festival and the history of ownership of the farm. She wore a multi-colored striped floppy hat, a long sleeve pullover with a bright floral skirt and boots. Her face was strong and handsome and she looked like Helga in Andrew Wyeth's famous series on his neighbor. She was very articulate. The upshot of all this activity was to arrange a meeting with the new owner to discuss camping on the site. The 28th anniversary of Woodstock was coming up in a month.

1997

CHAPTER 2

A BAD DAY IN PARIS

Ah, Paris! For me, it's a city of wine, women, excitement and beauty. But not always.

Nancy and I stopped off in Paris (a Father's Day gift from her) after a delightful sojourn in Istanbul. The dollar had been robust in Turkey, but we soon found it quite anemic in France.

We took the bus from the airport to Les Invalides and then taxied to our Left Bank hotel. The taxi was metered, but the meter only counts human beings. Luggage is in a special class and costs more for the one-mile ride than Nancy and I together — a lot more.

We paid and went into our hotel on the Rue Bonaparte. Nancy had seen this hotel on a previous visit to Paris, but, when we moved in, we understood all too well two common French words — petite and chér. The room was on the top floor, so part of the ceiling in this petite, chér room slanted down. We slouched to the bathroom.

For lunch, we went to a nearby restaurant. It was a little after two, just past Paris' lunch hour, but the waiter finally agreed to approach our table. I ordered the special — tomatoes, veal and dessert. Nancy said she just wanted soup and a plain salad. OK — why not? Well, the bill showed that her meal was quite a bit more expensive than my three-course lunch, which turned out to be two-courses because the waiter put on his coat and left before I got my dessert. The food? Well, it was below the standard fare in Turkey.

I needed a haircut and was sent by our hotel to a hair care establishment with a sign that read: "Mesdames & Messieurs." I entered into what appeared to be a beauty parlor. I was the only male customer. I told the proprietor I wanted a "light trim." He referred me to a not-very-happy gentleman in a bright blue shirt and a vivid orange vest who looked at me and spoke his only two words of English. "Him? Now?" "Oui."

The unhappy barber then beckoned me to go upstairs. He gave me a thorough shampoo — the first professional one I'd ever had. To me, his English was non-existent. My French on the subject of hair care is woefully weak.

Mr. Blue and Orange then took me downstairs to a chair next to a lady reading a novel. She knew my hair stylist and they chatted rapidly in French during my five-minute trim. The cost — $35 plus the expected tip — was not exactly the usual $9. The results — a hasty-looking French haircut which my wife failed to notice.

It was a damp, misty day and even a walk through my favorite park in the world — the Luxembourg Gardens — failed to raise our spirits to the level we were used to in Paris.

Our dinner, at a restaurant recommended by our swear-by red Michelin Guide, was a disaster. As we arrived, Nancy looked in and said, "The windows are dirty." I replied, "I'm starving." We went in. The restaurant was "decorated" with unfinished wooden walls with baskets of dried wheat and weeds. Reverse French chic, I guess. The wine was good, the food disappointing, and the bill exorbitant (the highest we'd ever paid). The waiter — a combination of indifference and intimidation.

The walk back along the Seine was a boost but we were glad to return to our petite, chér room to sleep and anticipate a brighter day tomorrow.

The next day we awoke to a sunny day and to the Paris which we had remembered.

1998

CHAPTER 3

DEATH AND HOT AIR

Seeing two men die did not diminish my interest in hot air ballooning. I wanted to take my wife and six friends to the Albuquerque Balloon Festival. They were all reluctant, so I decided to go alone and scout it out first.

The balloon festival, held in early October each year, features the ascension of over 600 hot air balloons of all shapes and colors. They must go up at sunrise because that is the best time for the safest air currents, light and steady. It is an overwhelming sight — thousands of people with hundreds of madly different balloons gently rising into the sky.

I arranged at my hotel to go for a sunrise ride with the Red Baron Pizza balloon, a dark red balloon lettered to advertise its product. Each balloon has a basket that holds the pilot, three to five passengers and the gas heating unit that creates the hot air to lift the balloon into the sky. No pizzas.

To ascend, the heater forces hot air into the balloon. The roar of the hot air heater is deafening, but the balloon does rise. The only control the pilot has is: heater on — up; heater off — down. The air currents determine the direction, and they can differ as the altitude changes.

Our pilot had years of air ballooning experience. That made a difference, as we were to see.

When the heater was off, it was delightfully quiet. The balloon gently sailed along — this time with hundreds of other balloons around us. Some were shaped like beer cans, batteries, Santa Claus, sneakers, castles, animals. Most were multi-colored or striped, in teardrop shapes, with small baskets suspended from the bottom. We floated along the Rio Grande River with our reflection mirrored in the water. It was a serene yet exciting experience. We could see mountains in the distance one way and the city of Albuquerque in the other, surrounded by what looked like colorful gumdrops.

On the ground, under each balloon, was a crew in a truck, following along as best they could, ready to help when the balloon lands, using walkie-talkies for communication.

We left the river and floated over nearby fields looking for a good place to land, a place where the crew in the truck could get to us, help stabilize the landing and then fold up the balloon in the back of the truck.

Landings can be tricky. A friend of mine broke his foot in a balloon landing. The pilot told us to bend our legs and hunker down, holding on to the side of the basket when we hit the ground. We touched down at a bit of an angle and bounced along several times before finally coming to rest. It wasn't smooth but it was quite breathtaking and loads of fun. No one was hurt.

As we were folding up the balloon, our pilot noticed a nearby balloon heading toward high electrical wires. The balloon hit the wires and burst into flames — about 200 feet off the ground. The two men in the balloon scrambled around to avoid the flames. We watched in horror as the men jumped or fell to the ground. A free fall from 200 feet is usually fatal and this was no exception. Our balloon crew members were all badly shaken, feeling incredulous and helpless.

It turned out that the two men who were killed did not have much experience ballooning and evidently did not see or could not avoid the deadly wires.

That was over ten years ago, but that scene — the beauty of the ride and the tragedy of the accident — is still vivid. However, at that point in time I was determined to take my wife and friends to New Mexico and have another go at ballooning and to enjoy the Southwest.

The Albuquerque-Santa Fé area abounds with fascinating sights and activities. The many pueblos and Native American experiences alone are worth the trip. I enjoyed a concert of the New Mexico Symphony Orchestra with its guests, the wonderful Canadian Brass. They played several numbers together and it was a memorable musical treat. The New Mexico Symphony had a beautiful young French horn player, who joined the Canadian Brass in a lively Basin Street number. It brought the house down.

I returned home excited about my experience and told my friends everything. Finally they agreed to come with me the following year. None had ever been up in a balloon, but all agreed to give it a try, some very reluctantly.

We arose before daybreak and were assigned to two balloons. Some of the women were shaking at first, but, once up in the air, everyone agreed it was exhilarating. No one was hurt and that year there were no serious balloon accidents.

To some in our group, it was the beginning and end of their ballooning careers. To a few of us, it whetted our appetites for more.

1998

CHAPTER 4

FOUR HOURS WAS NOT ENOUGH

Last year, Nancy and I sailed the Aegean and spent four hours on Santorini, a most spectacular island. I almost jumped ship so I could stay longer. However, my wife and her sister and husband were sailing on, so I relented and rejoined them. But I did vow to return at a more leisurely pace.

Santorini is a dramatic Greek island in the southerly Cycladic group. It is crescent-shaped — 10 miles long and 2½ miles wide, and was formed by an incredible volcanic eruption 3,000 years ago. Earthquakes have continued to hit the island — the last one in 1956. The result is a caldera with cliffs over 1,000 feet high, rising out of the sea and topped by stark white towns facing the Aegean.

Sailing up to Santorini is one of the great sights of Greece. The gray and black and red cliffs of the caldera loom abruptly from the dark blue Aegean Sea, with a line of white buildings on top like vanilla icing on a cake. After mooring, we swam off our vessel and were overwhelmed as we looked up at this island which rose with great drama and beauty from the water.

This year, my sister and her husband and friends took the same trip, sailing through the Greek isles. I decided this was my opportunity to return — fly to Athens, meet them in Santorini and show them the island as I remembered it, then stay on by myself for a few days to photograph and enjoy this Greek treasure. I made the trip a day before they were to arrive.

Thera is Santorini's main town and it is mobbed with tourists and gift stores. There seems to be more gold in the literally hundreds of jewelry stores than I had ever seen anywhere else. However, Oia, a smaller town on the western tip, is less crowded, more picturesque and allows no cars on its foot-smoothed marble-block streets. The brilliant sunsets, reflecting from the sea, make Oia's white-washed buildings turn gold and then orange.

My digs were one of the many cave-like lodgings in the side of the caldera facing the sea. There was a pool for swimming and each room had its own balcony for breakfast. The view down the colorful caldera, with sailing and fishing vessels in Aegean blue waters, was a stunning sight that changed with the light and the wind.

I rented a car so I could show my friends around, during their four hours on the island, and to see for myself as much of Santorini as possible. They arrived and were as enchanted as I by this Greek Aegean gem. Two of my friends were having leg problems, so the car eased things a bit as we drove out to Oia and the little port of Ammoudi. This port is just below Oia, and has red and gold and white fishing boats moored. Large sailing vessels are seen blowing by on the horizon. Outdoor cafés, serving fresh fish grilled to order and tangy Santorini wine, make this a tasty destination — especially at sunset, as this port faces west.

We spent time at Akrotiri, an archaeological dig on the south coast. This is a Bronze Age city, buried in ash from a mighty volcanic eruption and earthquake thousands of years ago. We were greatly surprised that, although there appeared to be a sizable area already uncovered, only a third of the city was, at this point, excavated. Akrotiri is thought by some to be Atlantis, the lost city written about by Plato. The Greek government is supporting the excavations but, due to monetary cutbacks by Athens, the work is progressing slowly.

A few hours is, as I found, not enough of Santorini, but my friends were soon off to their boat, on to Rhodes. I was free to explore the villages, beaches, tavernas and hidden sights.

Near Akrotiri are two interesting but remote beaches. The so-called "white" beach is actually littered with gray boulders and pebbles, and is a family beach with limited topless bathers. Just down the coast is the more colorful "red" beach. It is approached by a rather steep, rocky path and is a pink stone beach at the foot of dramatic red cliffs. The view of the red rocks, white umbrellas on a pink beach and the aquamarine Aegean lapping up makes an incredibly colorful panorama.

The seashores on the south side of the island are called black sand beaches. This means dark gray pebbles, hot sun, and bronzing, topless European women who, every once in a while, dip their toes in the warm Aegean. This is also an appealing sight.

The architecture on the island is eye-catching and is dominated by the churches. There are more than 200 Greek Orthodox churches in Santorini. Most of them are white with Aegean blue domes, topped by a cross. Many have a series of cascading bronze bells, open to the elements, with attached ropes dropping to the ground so they can be rung on appropriate holy days. Some of the churches look freshly painted and newly built. One in particular was a large, white structure with a series of seven domes and handsome, open-air bell towers — a most striking edifice. This church was on a plain near Parrissa Beach and the only activity I saw around it was a group of Swedes, in a painting class, sketching the church. We were told there are only about twenty priests on the island, so that on Sunday each priest travels from church to church to conduct Mass.

Another unique church was a small, three-domed building on top of a rocky promontory, with a tattered Greek flag waving in the breeze. Everywhere you look on the island are these stand-out churches with their sensuous white and blue curves topped by the Christian cross.

The people of Santorini? I never did get to know any Santorinians well. Most are in the tourist service trade. However, several made an impression. One was the "Fuji One Hour Photo" gal (is there a town in the civilized world that does not have a one hour photo store?). This young lady was a shy, but helpful, blonde, looking more Scandinavian than Greek. Her name was Natasa. She did an efficient job on my photos and guided me in selecting locations to photograph and places to eat.

I am not a great fan of Greek food. One evening, at Natasa's suggestion, I went to an Italian restaurant in Oia. The best part of this meal turned out to be the waitress, not the food. She was attractive and friendly and wore a colorful, low-cut, peek-a-boo dress with a black bra visible underneath. What really stood out was a tattoo on her right breast — a flying horse, Pegasus, I imagine. I did not ask. She had a pretty, round face and rosy cheeks. Her full, sensuous lips turned into a warm smile whenever she spoke to me. Being an inveterate photographer, I was dying to snap her picture, a memento of an interesting if not very tasty meal. Finally, at the end of the meal, I said to her, "I like to take pictures of waitresses who help me when I dine out. May I photograph you?" She hesitated and then said, "Sure, why not?" I took two shots. They both came out very well, although in one a startled male waiter is staring in the background. My shy friend in the photo store, after she developed the pictures, said the name of the waitress was Vaso (pronounced "Bah so"). I took a copy to Vaso. This time she was dressed in a brief, two-piece play outfit and she gave me another friendly smile.

The only women I saw who seemed to be interested in more than just being helpful were two ladies from Texas. They were walking up a steep hill and I gave them a ride. They had been drinking and appeared lonely for male companionship. No thanks.

You can still see the old Greek widows in their black dresses and shoes, walking slowly down the village streets. They have sad but determined looks on their faces and usually carry shopping bags, laden with breads, wine and kitchen necessities.

There are stop signs on the roads of Santorini, but I never saw a car stop at one. However, two young German women on a bicycle slammed into my car as I was stopped in a small traffic jam. No one was hurt.

Nancy did not wish to accompany me on this trip to Greece and traveling alone has some advantages, especially if you are a photographer. Santorini is a dream place for a photo bug. However, I missed my wife and hope she accompanies me on my next photographic safari.

When I got home and had my Santorini photos printed, I was asked to display them at the local library. The photos seemed to be quite well received and the most talked about picture was — you guessed it — of Vaso, the waitress.

1998

CHAPTER 5

THE KAREN RING-NECKS

We were travelling in northern Thailand near the Burmese border to visit some of the hill tribes. We had been visiting the Hmong tribe who live way up in the hills in quite primitive grass and bamboo huts. They are farmers who the government had weaned away from growing opium poppies to growing cabbages. (At least that's what our guide told us.) They were evidently quite prosperous with their pick-up trucks and TV antennas.

Now we were anxious to visit the Karen Red tribe, famous for its colorful women who wear multiple rings around their necks. I envisioned tall stately women with many rings on their elongated necks symbolic of some mysterious or sexual ritual.

The tribe lived even further up the hillsides, and we travelled in four-wheel-drive vehicles up shallow streams and over many riverlets until finally we arrived at a small settlement of *two* Karen tribes — the Red and the Blue. Had it been the rainy season, the only means of reaching the tribes would have been on elephants.

The Karen Blue are farmers and the Karen Red are farmers and weavers. It was the Karen Reds we wanted to visit because of the women with ringed-necks.

It was a hot day, over 100° F, and we walked very slowly over to a tidy row of well-maintained bamboo huts on either side of the road. The women and girls were sitting at tables selling trinkets and woven fabrics. They wore brass rings around their necks — I counted as many as 17 — fewer on the younger girls aged 10 or 12. Several had handkerchiefs between the top ring and their chins. They also had rings on their arms and ankles, and strange square hats with fabric hanging down over their shoulders. Most looked quite uncomfortable — hot and rigid. Instead of stately tribal people, they were rather pathetic — almost like freaks in a side show.

We bought some trinkets and a few woven scarves so we felt more at ease in taking our obligatory photos.

Other women there were in bright red blouses but no jewelry, and were industriously doing the weaving. All in all, it was not exactly as we had expected or been led to believe.

After we got back to America, the next issue of "National Geographic" had a story and picture of these women. We were told the original purpose for wearing the neck rings was to protect them from man-eating tigers. There are no tigers left in Thailand or nearby Burma — so now they wear this jewelry to attract tourists and make money from them. Even though they are off the beaten track, tourists come and the women make some money that way. We ultimately felt misled but we did see the Karen ring-necks. Should we really have expected more?

1998

CHAPTER 6

TIBET

I never visited a foreign region with as much anticipation as Tibet. Nancy and I went to China with a Dartmouth tour group and the highlight of the trip was a five-day stay in remote Tibet. Professor George Demko was our leader. He had been a geographer for the United States State Department. He liked Secretary Schultz and disliked Secretary Baker.

We flew from the lovely Chinese city of Chengdu in Szechuan Province (altitude 300 ft.) to exotic Lhasa in Tibet (altitude 12,5000 ft.). The flight itself was spectacular. We flew over parts of the Himalayas with their gigantic white snowy peaks and fingers of green valleys leading down to brown rivers.

We had been warned by our Chinese national guide not to enter into any political discussions or to talk about or give out pictures or materials on the Dalai Lama.

Tibet had been an independent country and closed to outsiders for many years. The People's Liberation Army of China occupied Tibet in 1951 and, after eight years of fruitless negotiations with Beijing, the Dalai Lama was forced to flee to India. The Tibetans are a peaceful and non-violent people as a result of their strict adherence to Buddhism. They tried their best to resist the Chinese, but their resistance only led to tragic results. Of seven million Tibetans, one million died due to Chinese oppression, suppression and terrorism. Over 2,000 Buddhist temples were destroyed. The Chinese now outnumber the Tibetans in Lhasa the capital.

The airport in Lhasa is the highest in the world (everything in Lhasa is "the highest in the world") and also one of the dirtiest and least organized.

We took a bus into Lhasa, passing the river people who were launching their yak-skin boats in the murky Lhasa River.

Our Tibetan guide was an attractive young lady, part Chinese, with a beautiful smile and a pleasant and helpful manner. The Tibetan people have jet-black hair, red cheeks and ruddy complexions. Their appearance reminded me a bit of Native Americans.

Out hotel, the Holiday Inn, is second rate but, for Tibet, a decidedly third-world region, first rate. Each of the rooms had an oxygen dispenser in case we couldn't catch out breath due to the altitude (two-and-one-half miles high). We took it very easy the first several hours, sometimes even days, adjusting. Several members of our group felt faint but recovered and most were acclimated in a day or two.

Unfortunately, that evening, Nancy became violently ill with nausea and a vicious headache. I was very concerned and finally fetched the hotel doctor, a Tibetan who served the Panchen Lama. He came to our room and gave Nancy bitter-tasting tea and some brownish pills. She had a very difficult night but was better in the morning.

I learned from Professor Demko, who had also seen this doctor, that he was a diagnostic whiz. Curious, I went to see him the next day. He looked like a bigger version of Deng Xiaoping and had a very cordial manner. He diagnoses a patient's health by feeling the pulse. This is based on the medieval theory of humors, blood, bile and phlegm in the body.

Through his interpreter, the doctor asked me one question: "How is your sex life?" I murmured something about the altitude and that it wasn't too good. I asked why he had asked that question. He said he detected a problem with my kidney which could have affected my sex life. I told him I had a kidney stone attack several weeks ago. He also suggested that my digestive system was unstable, which I readily confirmed. He told me everything else was fine. He gave me some rabbit pellets, at least that's what they looked like, to aid my digestion. No western doctor I've told about this interesting and correct diagnosis believes the story.

The next day the rest of our group went on a two-day bus trip to the countryside. Due to Nancy's weakened condition, we stayed behind. I went down the road to Norbulinka, the park where the Dalai Lama had his Summer Palace. Fortunately, there was a harvest festival and Tibetans were coming from all over the countryside to picnic and celebrate. It was one of the most interesting times in my travels. The day was warm and sunny and people on bikes, horses, motorcycles, trucks and buses were pouring in, many wearing distinctive outfits from their regions.

I remember one beautiful young woman with gold in her teeth and a terrific smile. She wore turquoise and amber jewelry in her hair and around her neck, and a black and white cape with a colorful sash. Tibetan women are known to wear their dowries. Some of the men were from the Khampa Region — tall, fierce-looking men with red or black scarves rolled and tied on their heads, wearing capes with sashes. They looked like bandits and the story has it that, out in the countryside, they are in fact bandits. They put up the strongest resistance to the Chinese and many Khampas were slaughtered.

There were other groups of men in fedoras and Western dress, sitting on brightly woven rugs in a circle of fifteen with several hundred beer bottles in the center.

The most impressive were the many families sitting by multi-colored tents and hanging cloths. The tents had designs of monkeys, elephants, cranes and other attractive patterns. They had brought their dinner, usually *tsampa* made of barley flour, and a colorful thermos of yak tea. I will not forget their gracious smiles as they asked me to join them and share a cup of yak tea — warm, salty and bitter. We communicated only through gestures but I was touched by their friendliness and sharing. I don't believe they ever understood where I was from but I did enjoy the companionship of a number of beautiful Tibetan families.

Later Nancy was feeling better and she and I walked over to the Dalai Lama's Summer Palace, a two-story structure surrounded by golden statues and colorful banners. We went inside for a tour. Each room was brightly painted in reds, yellows, oranges and blues. Some rooms had pictures of the Dalai Lama and people were prostrate in front of them, putting money in baskets.

It was quite hot and very crowded in the palace. There was a long line to get to the second floor bedrooms. As we waited, a path opened for us and we went to the head of the line. We may have been the only Westerners there and were treated like welcome guests.

It is said that most Tibetans bathe only once a year. Thus, I was amazed that, although we were packed in closely with the group in the Summer Palace, the air seemed clean and pure. I later learned that because Tibet is so high, both the cold temperatures and the sun's ultraviolet rays act as sterilizers, killing most bacteria. The result is even though most Tibetans are dirty by western standards, they are healthy and are actually cleaner than they appear.

Beautiful flowers and gardens were planted in front of the palace and many people were milling about. A photographer was taking pictures of small groups, with the lovely palace in the background. I was able to jump in and get some memorable pictures of Tibetans, especially brightly dressed children in front of their treasured palace.

We went through the Summer Palace twice. It was full of color and Tibetan art and Buddhist artifacts. It had the look and feel of the place that the Dalai Lama was forced to abandon 33 years ago. The beautiful views from his bedroom to the hills and mountains in the distance made it a home much loved by the Dalai Lama.

In the center of the same park was a stage where the Tibetan opera company performed. They were dressed in silk brocade costumes and wild spirit masks. They danced and sang in what sounded like a moaning chant. Nearby a man was attempting to cure the aches and pains of another by placing his hands several inches from the affected area and trying to draw the bad Karma out and replace it with good Karma. There was a line of people waiting their turns to be cured.

The University of Tibet had a booth at this harvest festival. They sold mandala-type paintings and attractive yak jewelry, both of which we purchased. The young lady at this booth spoke some English. Oddly enough, she was the only Tibetan who refused to be photographed when I asked.

The city of Lhasa now has a strong Chinese influence with shopping stalls along the main street and barracks to house the many Chinese. However, the city is still dominated by the main palace, the Potala, situated on a hill near the center.

The Potala is thirteen stories high, one-quarter mile wide and can be seen for miles around. It has over 1,000 rooms and was the principal residence of the Dalai Lama, although he preferred the Summer Palace. Both palaces were spared from Chinese destruction by the intercession of Chou En Lai. The Potala, too, is bright with colors, red carved doorways and golden statutes. It has rooms with sumptuous golden tombs of earlier Dalai Lamas. It is a remarkable building and is shown with great pride by the Tibetan guides.

In the Tibetan section of Lhasa are two-story apartments with red and blue designs painted on them. Atop each apartment and displayed in profusion all over the city are prayer flags of different colors with sacred prayers written on them.

The next day the guide took us into the countryside to see the Gander Monastery. This trip wound through a lovely, peaceful valley to the foothills of the Himalayas. Gander is on the side of a mountain at 14,500 feet. It had been destroyed by the Chinese and was recently rebuilt. There were numerous monks with their shaved heads and their maroon robes — chanting and praying and singing. Nancy had a tape recorder and recorded their voices. When she played it back for them, they burst into joyous laughter and were quite taken by my wife and her magic machine.

Our Dartmouth tour group picnicked on Jarmalinka Island in the middle of the Lhasa River. To get to the island, we crossed a bridge draped with thousands of prayer flags. A Chinese vendor was there to sell prayer flags as we crossed.

From the island we watched Tibetan men washing rugs and clothing in the muddy river, and across the river, we could see the entrancing Potala, looming over Lhasa with the Himalayan mountains in the background. It was our last day in Tibet and we enjoyed every minute.

Our guides had left us and no one else was on the island. Professor Demko was able to give an open and candid lecture on the politics and problems of beleaguered Tibet.

We were sad to leave this "Tibetan Region," in such a glorious part of the world, with its beautiful people and life-enhancing Buddhist traditions. It was, of course, even sadder to see what the Chinese had done and were continuing to do in their subtle and not-so-subtle attempts to bring this great and ancient society in line with the aims of the Chinese government.

1995

CHAPTER 7

W.D.

Question #1: What 20th century artist has given the most pleasure to the most people? Picasso? Matisse? Brancusi? Monet? Dr. Seuss? NO, NO, NO, NO, NO. My answer is Walt Disney.

Question #2: What is one of the truly great joys of life after 40-50-60-70-80? Travel, eating, sex, religion, gardening? NO, NO, NO, NO, NO. My answer is grandchildren.

And, if you put the two together, Disney and grandchildren, you have a treat par excellence.

Nancy and I took our five grandchildren and the two mothers (divorced) with us for two and one-half days to Disney World. All nine of us had a ball! This Disney theme park has got to be one of the best-run enterprises anywhere. As a businessman, I marvel at Disney's ability to continually please its guests and anticipate their needs, wants and pleasures. Their cast members, as they call them, and other Disney workers that you meet, are all very friendly, helpful and most anxious to please. At a "character breakfast," Goofy came over to our table, signed his autograph and teased with Annie and Liz — then posed several times with them for the "I met Goofy" pictures. And the cleaning maid in our room was very friendly and helpful, and made sure our stay there was all we could hope for.

Our luau at the Polynesian Village was a big hit. All nine of us devoured our meal with great raves and delight — ribs and chicken, stir-fried vegetables, fresh fruit — simply delicious, which is not easy for a group of several hundred.

The luau show featured Mickey, Minnie, Goofy, hula dancers, mermaids and brawny "Hawaiian" men — a treat for all.

Since the ages of the grandchildren ranged from 3 to 12 — 3, 6, 8, 9, 12 — we found it easier to split up and go at an appropriate pace to the interests of each child. It also had the advantage of giving Nancy and me the chance to be alone with one or two of the grandchildren at a time.

Three-year-old Kimmie's main interest was the characters — especially Minnie and Mickey. She was quite thrilled to wait in line, get their signatures in her book and then pose with them. The older children all seemed to be most excited by the thrill rides — Space Mountain, Splash Mountain and the Tower of Terror — long lines for each. And we all enjoyed the wonderful, funny and amazing 3-D Muppet Show.

On a hot afternoon, seven of us went to a water park, "Typhoon Lagoon." It was mobbed. After I let Nancy out of our car — we had two cars — I struggled to find a parking space. They had to open a new parking area to accommodate the crowd. By the time I got in the park, all I could see was a mass of thousands of swimsuit-clad people. Since we had not designated a meeting spot, I couldn't find our group. I walked around for an hour or so, looking and snapping pictures. They have a large lake with a plastic and sand beach, every inch filled with Disney guests. Every five minutes, a large wave is generated at the far end of the pool that causes shrieks of delight from all the leaping and diving bathers as it goes to the beach. And there are water slides and long, inflated tube rides on a slowly moving run. I enjoyed watching the beach revelers but never found my family and finally left.

At night, we went to the "Main Street Electrical Parade." Liz, eight-years-old, described this as "awesome." Five hundred miles of twinkling lights make this another dazzling bit of Disney magic. All the costumes and floats were festooned with these lights and it did draw an "awesome" response from all the children (and big kids, too — we're all kids at Disney World).

One of my favorite spots is Team Disney headquarters — it used to be Disney International headquarters. The building is one of the most delightful bits of architecture I've ever seen. In the center is a high silo-like structure in beige and deep pink — open at the top— that serves as a sundial inside. In front of this is a red cube, sitting on a wonderful bright pink building. The sides are tall, reddish-purple buildings on either side and these are flanked by long four-story, soft gray and pink office buildings, each with 72 large, square windows. This — in the back — is all overlooking a large reflecting lake. The overall effect is a delight to the eye. I asked several people who worked there if they liked the building and got a very positive response. The architect is Japanese — Aroki. The building is not on the normal visitor tour but is worth a look. It is across the way from "Planet Hollywood."

The grandchildren (and their mothers and grandparents) enjoyed every bit of D.W. They did get a little tired and cranky after a long, hot day. But, for the most part, we would see their eyes light up with anticipation and joys at all the many colorful and exciting delights of D.W.

Three cheers for Walt Disney! The most pleasing artist and entrepreneur of our time.

1998

CHAPTER 8

MORE W.D.

We returned to Disney World once again with our grandchildren. This was about two months after Animal Kingdom, a new Disney addition, opened.

The story is that Michael Eisner, CEO of Walt Disney Corporation, was lukewarm about an animal park. "Would throngs come to see wild animals in Florida?" An associate, enthusiastic about the possibility, brought a live tiger on a chain to Eisner's office and paraded the animal around. The hair stood up on Eisner's neck. He was persuaded to go for it.

When the Animal Kingdom opened in '98 the initial reviews were tepid. Some of the animals died and the Disney skeptics were smiling.

Several months ago, Nancy and I returned from a trip to South Africa which included five exciting days on safari. Thus we were very leery about what Disney could do to compete with our African experience.

We were told by fellow visitors at Disney World that the crowds at the Animal Kingdom were massive by midday. And we had learned in Africa that wild animals were more active early in the morning or late in the day. They often sleep during the midday heat. We got up at 6 a.m. and arrived at the Animal Kingdom as it opened at 7 a.m.

First we went to "It's Tough to be a Bug," a lively 3-D presentation. We got spit at, pinched, stung, stunk-up and shocked —all in feelable simulations — which left us jumpy but with exhilarated smiles on our faces. Three cheers for Disney's bugs! On to live animals!

We went to the Kilimanjaro Safari — waited in line 30 minutes — watching an animal video about hippos fighting — lions, etc. Finally we boarded a safari truck and were off to see the animals "in the wild." We soon saw four hippos — a mother and a baby half submerged and two large males fighting — as in the video. We went on to see two lions, three cheetahs, six elephants, three white rhinos and assorted antelopes — all in African-appearing settings and easily viewable. We were all excited by our 20-minute safari ride and couldn't have asked for more — in that short period and in Central Florida bush. After we walked a "forest exploration trail," where we encountered exotic and colorful African birds in a well-disguised aviary, we soon spotted a troop of lowland gorillas, cavorting in trees and hilly grasslands. We watched open-mouthed at these playful primates. Still yet to come was a "maharajah jungle trek," said to feature tigers and Komodo dragons. I had recently read about the possibilities that tigers in the wild could soon be extinct because of their predilection for killing humans. I was most anxious to see what Disney had done. We were not disappointed. The tigers, a mother and six large but young females, frolicked together and put on quite a show for us enthusiastic watchers. They chased each other and bit the backs of their siblings' necks and splashed in a large puddle of water. What fun for us and for these largest of the "big cats." They seemed to have plenty of room to roam and play. The key to seeing them is to go between 8 and 9 in the morning or 6 and 7 at night. Otherwise, like lions, they sleep a lot during the day. What magnificent creatures they are. A Disney guide told our grandchildren that Mickey Mouse protects us from the tigers. And the Komodo dragon spit out his yellow forked tongue at us, he being a 6-foot long lizard with a reputation as a man-eater.

The grandchildren's reactions to all this was the well-worn but enthusiastically descriptive "awesome!" We realized that this was, of course, a glorified zoo but the animals appeared as if in the wild, seemed to have lots of open space and looked well off in their new habitat.

Controversial though it may be, for us, Disney had done it again. Disney continues to do what it does so well — bring joy, pleasure, and excitement to so many people. We can't wait to return.

1999

CHAPTER 9

OLYMPIAN VISITS

It was 1948 and I was out of the Army and back at Dartmouth when I decided to study at the Sorbonne in Paris for the summer. I was studying French and always wanted to go to Paris. Why not study there for a semester? The G.I. Bill was paying my way at Dartmouth.

I lasted one day at the Sorbonne. There were only Americans in my class and I wanted more of a European experience. I enjoyed the splendors of Paris and then toured France ending up in London to see the 1948 Olympic games. The first post-war games since 1936 in Berlin which were remembered for two people, Adolph Hitler and Jesse Owens.

I got a room in the Chelsea section of London and then went to the local pub for a warm beer. The bartender was very friendly and invited me to meet her daughter, Fiona. Fiona was a chubby English lass who had evidently been too young to meet American G.I.'s during the war. She was round-faced with flashing eyes and was anxious to finally meet a young American. We went to the dance movie "The Red Shoes" and later, over some beers, talked about ballet, sports and dating. My relationship with Fiona was intense but short-lived because at that point, I was more interested in meeting some Olympic athletes.

A close friend at Dartmouth had gone to Andover with Jimmie McLane, the world-class American swimmer. I went to his event, the 1500-meter swim, saw him win and then went up to him and had a long and candid chat. He was a handsome young sixteen-year-old. McLane talked about the water being cold. It was an outdoor pool, the summer had been cool and the water was not heated. The event had been sparsely attended and, of course, no TV cameras and not much press. Today, because of security and the media, an impromptu conversation with an athlete would be impossible.

At the track and field I was able to get good close-up pictures of Mel Patton, the winner of the 200-yard dash and Harrison Dillard, whom the papers called "That Negro from Baldwin-Wallace College" and winner of the 100-meter (10.3 seconds).

I also recall seeing Emil Zatopec of Czechoslovakia — the balding winner of the 10,000-meter run. He was a big favorite with the Europeans. Zatopec was a Czech army officer who was promoted right after he won. After the Olympics two Czechs and three Hungarians defected by refusing to leave London, but not Zatopec who went home to the army.

As early as in the 1948 Olympics there were rumors of performance-enhancing drugs and the suggestion was made to give the athletes blood tests.

Even a touch of terrorism was felt. As the Olympic torch was being carried from Athens to London, armed insurgents in Greece threatened the safety of the runners. Nothing serious came of it.

Only about 60 nations participated in the 1948 Olympics. Notable among the absentees were Russia ("declined to go"), Israel (forced out by the Arabs), Germany and, amazingly, all of Africa and Asia.

It was a wonderful time for me, especially getting close to the athletes. It sure beat sitting in a Paris classroom with American students.

Forty-eight years later in 1996, the summer Olympics came to Atlanta, Georgia. I watched the games with great interest on TV and wondered how they compared with 1948. The first reports from Atlanta were high heat and humidity, slow and crowded transportation, no empty rooms, sold out events and then a bomb that killed two people. I decided to go.

My wife was incredulous. She thought I was absolutely crazy. Two close friends had just come back from the first days of the Olympics. We called them and they gave a glowing report. Nancy relented and I quickly took off for Atlanta — alone.

On my fifth call, I lucked into a lovely hotel room near the airport and subway. As I was requesting a jitney to the subway, an attractive young woman asked if she could go along. She was slim and blonde and quiet and serious. We traveled together directly to the center of Atlanta. She was pleasant and we talked. I found out she was a physician, originally from Kansas City, who had spent time in both West and East Africa. This was her day off and she was going to the Olympic art exhibit at the Art Center. I debated going with her but couldn't wait to get out and see the Olympic scene. I later regretted that decision. She seemed like a bright and delightful person and it would have been fun to see the exhibit with her. I did go later, alone, and found it an exceptional collection. There were two Van Goghs, which I had never seen before. They were magnificent and well worth the trip, but I missed seeing them with someone. I never got the young doctor's name or saw her again.

After a tour of the very colorful Coca-Cola-red pin-trading park and center with refreshing fountains and mountains of Olympic pins, tee shirts and hats, I decided to go see the Dream Team.

The Dream Team game against Croatia was sold out but a scalper happened to have a $15 ticket for only $70. The $15 seat was high above Atlanta. I had thought the Dream Team were tall men; from where I sat Shaquille O'Neill, 6'11", was reduced to a midget.

The United States led by 15 before I sat down, and the game was very one-sided. By the second half there were plenty of empty seats near the court. The Dream Team looked sloppy but the Croatians were helpless. The final score was

102-68 and the game was over in 70 minutes. That's a dollar a minute to see some of the best players in the world (and where was Michael Jordan?)

Six minutes from the end of the game a commotion erupted in the stands. It turned out to be the arrival of that famous "author," the orange-haired Dennis Rodman. He did not make the Dream Team, but he did make a dramatic entrance and exit.

My top priority was track and field and I was not disappointed. They had events in the morning — I sat in the shade — and in the evening; the hot afternoon sun had set. It was a beautiful new stadium, festooned with the colors of 197 nations, the eternal flame, the handsome brick-colored track and the world's top track and field athletes from all over the world: Burundi, Namibia, Ethiopia, Mozambique, Zambia, Uganda and South Africa were a few of the countries that produced outstanding runners. (Nigeria won the gold in the world's most popular sport — soccer). I was thrilled by the tall, thin woman representing France, Marie-José Perez, who came from Guadeloupe and lived in L.A. She won two gold medals and when she stood on the winners' stand to accept her medal, they played "The Marseillaise." I had shivers of joy.

Some people say you can see the Olympics better on TV. That may or may not be true. However it reminds me of sex. Nothing beats being there.

The evening events featured Carl Lewis and Michael Johnson, the best of the USA. The long jump was especially interesting. Both Lewis and Mike Powell, the world record holder, ended up face down in the pit. Lewis flopped down in stunned joy after he had seen how far he had leaped. Powell lay belly down in the sand for five minutes after he jumped. He had hurt himself, did poorly, and was out of medal contention.

There were lots of freebies in Atlanta to keep the people cool and happy, free cups of water, fans, cool sprays and even free subway rides if you showed your Olympic ticket. I had my picture taken free with a lovely southern belle. When I was given the picture the folder said, "Lord Jesus, I need you. Thank you for dying on the cross for my sins" from Aglow International. Later I noticed many religious signs and proselytes along the streets. "Repent, repent. Jesus Christ is coming soon. This is a warning — repent or perish!" I was having a wonderful time and didn't want to repent or perish.

I chatted with the congenial people riding the subways. One African-American lady invited me to come to her restaurant for a meal. A white woman across from me was talking to a young black man. When he got off the train her husband admonished her for being so friendly. He said, "Be careful who you talk to — all kinds of people are here."

The only other sour note I encountered was when I asked a tall young German tourist with a two-day beard what he thought of Atlanta. He shrugged and then said quite loudly, "I do like all the babes!" Two young black women looked at him with daggers.

A final conversation with the African-American airport shuttle bus driver was more revealing.

Kim - "How do you like living in Atlanta?"

Jeff - "I love it!"

Kim - "Why?"

Jeff - "Everyone is always so friendly. It's not just for the Olympics but all the time. I moved here from New Jersey. Right away I found the people here wonderful. I wouldn't leave."

(We passed a sign to Birmingham)

Kim - "Do you think this friendliness is true in Birmingham, too?"

Jeff - "I haven't been there but probably. This niceness seems to be catching on all over the South."

As far as Atlanta is concerned all I can say is "Amen."

1996

CHAPTER 10

SAFARI

A Walk in the Bush

I had often dreamed of a walk in the wild bush of Africa. We were staying in a game park near Kruger Park in South Africa and our ranger, Rowan, suggested a walk after breakfast. Rowan was a 22-year-old, large, ruddy-faced, white South African farm boy with a crew cut, enthusiastic and knowledgeable about African wild life. He was just back from a vacation and was a bit of an energetic cowboy.

He said we'd walk for an hour looking at "some of the smaller details of life in the bush - paw prints, birds, beatles and dung - a kind of a poop walk." We drove a mile or so in the Land Rover and then got out to walk along a dirt road. The day before we had seen several lions walking on such a road in the Park. Rowan said, "Stick close to me. It's doubtful there will be any predators around but we have to be careful." He was carrying a rifle and had the native trooper drive the Land Rover about 200 yards behind us.

We saw rhino tracks as big as dinner plates, and baboon tracks that looked like human hand prints. Colorful carmine bee eater birds perched nearby. A tall male giraffe stared at us over an acacia tree.

After walking a few hundred yards in the hot sun, we heard the loud cry of a baboon ahead of us. Rowan said, "Sometimes this means a predator is nearby, but it's probably only a call between mates." The baboon cry persisted and Rowan repeated his words about the possibility of a predator or a mating call, but he had a nervous scowl. The baboons kept screaming and finally Rowan motioned the Land Rover forward and told us quietly but firmly to "get in the vehicle quickly." We obeyed without hesitation. Just then another Land Rover came toward us and the driver said, "There are six lions just around the corner and down the hill."

We proceeded in that direction and shortly saw six lions lying in the sand under a tree, some simply looking around and a few fast asleep. They were two young males and four females. Their stomachs did not look full but they did not appear ready to stalk some prey.

That brought an end to our walking safari, but we did get some memorable photos and had a few nervous laughs.

We had been told that if a lion approaches you when you're walking - stop - DO NOT RUN. "Stand your ground and nine chances out of ten the lion will stop before reaching you, and will back away." The rangers we met each claimed they had had this experience. It was not an experience we really wanted to test. But we would certainly remember our "walk in the bush."

The Thieving Leopard

It was early morning and we had seen a dead impala slumped about forty feet up in the crotch of a tree. The impala had been killed by a leopard and left in the tree for a later meal. Leopards are solitary animals and seldom stay together except to mate or train a cub.

Meanwhile, we saw a female leopard. She had spotted this meal in the tree and was lying nearby in the thickets. Vultures were circling overhead so Rowan said this leopard would try to steal the impala before the birds got it.

We had driven close to this predator and near the tree. The leopard started to growl softly. Rowan told us the leopard was warning us not to come between her and her meal. We went no further.

The leopard crouched on the ground and finally slowly inched her way to the base of the tree. She looked up and then, in a flash, climbed the forty feet to the impala. She grabbed it with her mouth, lifted it up and backed down the tree. She then took her prey into a heavy thicket — disappearing from sight and preparing for her meal.

We took some exciting pictures of this whole scene and were exhilarated by this crime in the jungle.

Tracking Lions

We went out one morning to track lions so we could get some good photos of these majestic animals. We were in a Land Rover, which is a large, rugged, open-sided and topless vehicle. We were told we'd be fine as long as we didn't stand up or get out.

Lions are tracked by looking for paw prints on a dirt road or peering into the bush for movement or other clues. Our ranger, Gavin, was determined to find us a lion. We were driven around the area for several hours without much luck. When our Zulu tracker, Sofise, pointed in a certain direction, Gavin forged ahead into the heavy bush — knocking over thorn bushes, small trees and whatever was in our way. Our "safari tank" was relentless. Finally, Sofise noticed some tracks on the road which led into the heavy bush. Gavin and Sofise got out and said, "We're going to look around — we'll be back in ten minutes." Off they walked, Gavin with his rifle and Sofise with his sharp, dark eyes.

We waited —10 minutes, 15 minutes, 20 minutes. In a semi-serious way, we tried to decide what we'd do if they didn't return in 45 minutes or an hour or if we heard disturbing sounds — snarling, shouting or shooting. Where were we and where would we go? Who would drive? Finally, after more than thirty minutes, Gavin and Sofise walked out into the clearing with dejected looks. No lions. We had been tracking lions for three and a half hours and found none. However, as we returned to camp, we felt alive and strangely satisfied.

A few nights later, we went out tracking lions in the dark. This time, Rowan and Mangalese were our crew. Our tracker, Mangalese, sat in back of the Land Rover with a searchlight. Mangalese is a black South African of the San tribe with extremely keen eyes. We stopped periodically so he could relieve himself and have a smoke. We later learned that he had malaria.

Mangalese noticed fresh tracks and we came upon two large male lions — one on each side of the road. The one on the left walked down a short way to a small water hole. We followed him and, with our light on him, took photos as he took a long drink of water. He had a handsome mane and a raw sore below his left eye.

The lion on the other side of the road started to roar and move into the thick bush. We decided to follow him. Rowan said he was a lion unfamiliar to him and was probably not used to a stalking vehicle. However, the Land Rover crashed through the heavy bush and thickets to get closer to this big cat. Some of us became a little apprehensive. What if we cornered him in some impenetrable bushes or trees? And what if we got a flat tire? Would we all have to get out while Rowan and Mangalese fixed it in the dark? Rowan seemed unconcerned and we plowed on for ten minutes in this dark, dense bush. We did hear a muffled roar in the distance but never sighted the lion. So we drove back to the road and saw the wounded-eye lion lying on the side of the road, his thirst thoroughly quenched.

The next morning in the same area, we came across the same two lions lying near each other under a tree. It is said that lions sleep about 21 out of 24 hours. We were fortunate to have seen them the night before up and about.

One time we were looking for lions in Phinda, a private game reserve in Zuzuland. Phinda is a famous (or infamous) camp because one of its guests had been attacked and killed by a lion. The risk is that at night, if you leave your cottage for the main camp, you must call for an armed guard to escort you. This guest had neglected to do that. A fatal mistake. However this made Phinda all the more exciting to visit.

We had been driving and tracking along a hot, dusty road. As we rounded a bend, there, only fifty yards ahead and walking toward us, was the King, a large, solitary, heavily-maned lion. The "King of Phinda" as Gavin called him. Gavin quickly pulled over to the side so the lion wouldn't be chased away. The King went into the bush anyway but kept coming our way, passing our vehicle less than ten yards distant. He paid us scant attention as he padded by and the cameras were clicking like crazy. A wonderful photo-op.

The sight of that majestic lion walking on the road toward us so unexpectedly will remain with us a long time.

1999

CHAPTER 11

HIROSHIMA

8:15 a.m. August 6, 1945. That moment changed the course of the history of the world. That was the instant the first atomic bomb, "Big Boy," was detonated over Hiroshima, killing 100,000 people almost instantly and causing the deaths of another 100,000 during the next ten years. The bomb was delivered by the Enola Gay, an American B29 bomber. The Japanese called these bombers "Mr. B."

I was stationed at Camp Rucker in Alabama at the time, training as an infantryman in preparation for the proposed invasion of Japan. The Japanese were famous as fierce and determined defenders of their homeland, and it was estimated that as many as a million Allied casualties would result from the invasion. Further, more than one million Japanese could very well have died in the attempt to repel the invaders. Two million dead and wounded in this military operation was a strong possibility. And I might have been one of them.

When we heard the news of the detonation of the atomic bombs over Japan and finally of the Japanese surrender, our infantry unit was naturally ecstatic. I remember getting roaring drunk that night.

Fifty-five years later we visited Japan with a Dartmouth study group, and four of us, out of 28 in the group, decided to spend a day in Hiroshima. Today Hiroshima is an attractive and prosperous city of over a million people. It has wide streets, trees and parks and seven rivers running through it.

We took the bullet train from Kyoto to Hiroshima, almost 400 miles, and we were there in just under two hours. It was a beautiful sunny March day. From the station we taxied through to the Peace Park and got out on a bridge over the Ota-Gawa River. The wreckage of the A-bomb Dome, which had previously been the Industrial Promotion Center, is on the opposite bank. The dome is a grotesque skeleton of steel and brick left as was it was after the blast 55 years ago.

On the other side of the river is the Children's Memorial, a poignant and heart-rending statue of a young girl in the air surrounded by a vividly colorful sight — artwork and posters and literally millions of folded paper cranes in every hue — all created by Japanese school children.

The story, we learned, was about a ten-year-old Japanese girl, Sadako, who contracted leukemia from the atomic radiation. Cranes stand for long life and happiness in Japanese culture and she believed that if she folded 1000 paper cranes she would be cured. She folded 954 cranes and then died. Her schoolmates folded the rest and soon the tradition caught on with children throughout Japan. Now the colorful origami cranes are sent to the Children's Memorial and other atomic bomb shrines in the Peace Park. The four of us could hardly stop photographing these rainbow reminders of the thousands of children who perished on that most fateful day.

We eventually walked through the Park and past the Peace Flame — an ever-burning fire which will be extinguished only when the last nuclear weapon on earth is destroyed. Later we came to the Memorial Cenotaph, which contains the names of those killed by the bomb and carries the hopeful phrase, "Repose Ye in Peace, for the Error Shall Not Be Repeated."

We followed the broad path to the Peace Memorial Museum passing attractive fir trees. As expected the Museum hit us hard. First we watched a 20-minute video on the dropping of both atomic bombs and the immediate and long-term effects of the blasts. It was graphic and made me avert my eyes a number of times. There was no laying of blame but the video was unremitting in depicting the gruesome dying and deaths from radiation and multiple fire-related injuries. Many of the people who died in the initial blast have never been identified because of the total destruction at the center of the blast. In spite of extensive efforts to name all the victims, tens of thousands are known only to God.

The memorial video stunned us. Eventually we rose and toured the rest of the Museum. We saw a mock-up of a square mile of Hiroshima before the explosion, and then after — a complete wasteland. The exhibit showed watches stopped at 8:15, charred bodies, clothes and buildings and some granite steps that have a dark shadow — where someone had been sitting. The shadow was all that remained of that person after the blast.

When we had arrived in the Park early in the day it was almost deserted. Now the Museum was filling up with hundreds of uniformed school children, all crowding around the exhibits. They had paper and pencil and were taking notes — evidently a class assignment. We wondered what the reaction of these children would be to Americans among them. We found that in the Museum we were virtually ignored, as if we weren't there. Outside the Park it was a different story. As the children sat on the ground taking notes or eating lunch, we tentatively approached them and asked for a chance to photograph them. They seemed eager and pleased to pose for us and many gave us the peace sign as we snapped our shutters. We approached more and more groups and got warm responses, a few words of English, a high-five or handshake, shy smiles and giggles, and a chance to photograph each other with our arms around the children. Then there was the ever-present Japanese bowing. The children's teachers were equally agreeable. This was in sharp contrast to those tragic exhibits and movie we had seen inside. Life and hope go on even after the gravest of tragedies; children are the main conduit for our faith in the future.

Our stay in the Park, which lasted almost four hours, was much buoyed by the sight and interactions of these hundreds of children who had come to learn the lesson of the Hiroshima atomic bomb.

As we were leaving the Park we were stopped by two men who asked us to sign our names, addresses and ages on a petition to pledge to work toward peace and an end to atomic warfare. We signed eagerly and made the requested donation for the upkeep of the Peace Park.

I certainly shall never forget my visit to Hiroshima and pray that the horror "shall not be repeated."

2000

CHAPTER 12

AN INNOCENT ABROAD

My dentist's daughter is a poet, Priscilla Becker. Three of her poems were in the forty-fifth anniversary edition of "The Paris Review."

After reading her haunting poetry:

"...I take like wild vine to my bed.

And may I have a word with the miser measuring out my joy,"

I read an interview with Ned Rorem in the same issue. Rorem is a composer and writer who spent much of the fifties in Paris and wrote about it in "The Paris Diary." His friends in France were Jean Cocteau, Countess de Noailles, Julian Green and Janet Flanner. I lived in Paris during part of that period, and my friends were Sam, M'ree, Mme. Bernis and Therese and then Vera.

Sam was a graduate student I had met aboard ship sailing to France. We saw each other frequently in Paris. He was more forward and street-wise (or foolish) than I. When we took the Metro, Sam liked to make outrageous sexual remarks to the passing French girls. They ignored him. I would shrink away.

One day, Sam met a young lady in a public piscine (swimming pool). In the water, she proceeded to show him her private parts. He took her back to his apartment for the night. When he awoke the next morning she was gone along with his wallet.

Sam met a pert blonde prostitute named M'ree. She didn't overcharge him. We would lunch with her at an outdoor café in Montparnasse and laugh with her as she assessed each passing potential customer. "He ees no pay."

Mme. Bernis was the landlady of my apartment on the Rue de Rennes. She taught philosophy at the Sorbonne and spent summers at her country home in Normandy. She invited me to join her there for a weekend. Her country home was a lovely old stone farmhouse. She claimed that during the war German officers were billeted at her farmhouse and she never once spoke to them.

Mme. Bernis asked me my opinion of the Truman-Dewey presidential race in America. I told her I favored Dewey. "Il est plus intelligent." I didn't tell her that our family members were all Republicans. (At least at that time we were, and what ever happened to Tom Dewey?)

Mme. Bernis introduced me to her niece, Therese, a pretty, dark-haired Parisienne about my age. She was delightful to be with and I was enchanted. Sartre was the sensation of Paris then and we discussed him with more pleasure than passion. (I still don't understand existentialism.) However, I saw her only a few times as I had planned to travel south and visit the Riviera. I wrote Therese when I got home but never saw or heard from her again.

As a departing gift, Mme. Bernis gave me a pound of her fresh homemade Normandy butter. I took it all the way back to the States, and, needless to say, when I opened my suitcase to show my parents this gift from France it was rancid and had melted.

Hitchhiking to the Riviera, I ended up in Nice and soon went swimming on its stony beach. There I met Vera. She was a tall, shapely blonde in a smashing navy swimsuit who seemed to like Americans. We swam together and chatted together. She had been studying English and American literature, and I was majoring in English. Soon we were quoting Shakespeare to each other:

> Shall I compare thee to a summer's day?
> Thou art more lovely and more temperate.
> If music be the food of love, play on.

I was smitten.

Vera took me to a small café in old Nice where we had fried octopus. She then invited me to have dinner with her family the following night. She lived in Monte Carlo and her father was a retired Dutch sea captain. The dinner with her family was a most pleasant experience but I wondered how often she invited young men to meet the folks. My presence didn't faze her parents. However, her younger brother was in a caustic mood. "What's so good about the United States?"

Vera and I went out dancing and, as I took her home, I tried to kiss her. She said, "They do that so soon in America." They do and I did.

I had to leave Vera the next day for Italy and I was hopelessly in love. As I took the train from Monte Carlo to Florence I was floating ten feet off the ground.

We corresponded for a year or two. I sent her some American silk stockings and she sent me French perfume (for my mother). In one letter, she suggested that she might come to the United States. All that held her back was a $500 bond so she could get a visa. I didn't have the money and my father was not enthusiastic. "You'll end up marrying her and you'll regret it." That was close to the end of my relationship with Vera. My college roommate, Pierce, went to Paris the next year and saw her working in a night club as a cigarette girl. He saw her again once or twice before he, too, headed south. She ended up marrying the drummer in the night club band, a Cuban. The last we heard, Vera was living in Havana.

On the ship coming home, I met Claude, a young Parisian fille, on her way to an all-girl prep school in Connecticut. I was immediately attracted to her and we became inseparable on the ship. She was a short, sweet-faced brunette who exuded youthful innocence and naturalness. And she was French. (I had become a dedicated Francophile.)

Upon landing, I returned to Dartmouth. Claude and I promised to keep in touch.

One weekend on my way back from a Yale-Dartmouth football game I hitchhiked to her prep school. It was Halloween and they were having a party. Claude had been crying. The headmistress explained to me that the scary masks had frightened her — reminding her of the war days in Paris. I tried to comfort her but soon was advised it was time for me to leave. I wrote Claude suggesting we meet in New York City. Her headmistress would not allow it. That was the last of Claude.

Soon thereafter, my sister Priscilla who was also going to college in New Hampshire introduced me to her roommate — attractive, fascinating, lively Nancy. We dated off and on for two years and have been living together, mostly happily, for the last 50 years, as husband and wife.

1999

CHAPTER 13

SKIING AT SEVENTY

I believe in the 30-second rule. Most people like to talk about their health — especially as they get older and have more to talk about. The 30-second rule — seldom followed — is that no one should talk about his or her health problems for more than 30 seconds. This helps prevent eyes glazing over, boredom, indifference and loss of contact.

So, here's my 30 seconds. I have coming and going arthritis, special occasion high blood pressure, toenail degeneration, a Zantac-demanding stomach, skin cancers caused by teenage romping in the sun and no spleen. Except for stamina, I feel about 45, although I am 70 plus. And I still enjoy skiing.

We ski together as a family — my sister and her husband and children, and Nancy and our six children, and their families. This year we all decided to go to Stowe, Vermont.

The day before we left, I stopped to see my dermatologist. (Actually, she is my fifth dermatologist — and, I hope, my last.) On the way to the car after my appointment, my feet went out from under me on a sheet of ice and I landed hard on my back and head. I was stunned for a moment and couldn't catch my breath. I started back toward the doctor's office for help but soon started breathing easier and decided to drive home and rest. I had been planning to shop for snow tires to combat the snows of Vermont but, at that moment, it was out of the question.

At home, I groaned and wheezed to a friend who was helping us house clean, but soon I felt better. I did not have a headache, although it had been a sharp blow to my head. However, my back was so sore I could barely stand straight. That night I had trouble sleeping because it pained me whenever I moved. That was how I started on our ski trip.

Nancy and I took a granddaughter, 11-year-old Trish, in the car with us up to Stowe. She is happy and chatty, and was a most welcome passenger up to Vermont. But, needless to say, a sore, sensitive back does not add to one's desire to get on the ski slopes right away.

After a couple of days of groaning whenever I stood up, I decided it was time to ski. I went to the base lodge and got some lunch. It hurt my back just to carry the tray but, since the weather forecast was poor for the next few days, I went down and rented skis for one-half day. The ski rental man said, "I hope I can ski at 70." I replied, "And why not?" He said, "The knees — the knees." I didn't tell him I felt like an achy 45-year-old.

It was foggy, windy and spitting frozen rain at the top of the lift, but my back seemed okay and I could concentrate on "keep your weight on the downhill ski and relax! Keep skis parallel" — all the things I'd tried for years. I attempted to get into a relaxed rhythm on the slopes by singing "Tea For Two." The rain increased, so, after several hours, that was it for the first day.

That night it rained and washed away much of the snow. The next day, sloppy as it was, I took the five grandchildren to the tour of the Ben and Jerry Ice Cream factory. We all got a big kick out of that and ended up having our favorite flavors as a treat before leaving. And I did learn that in driving, it's better to separate sisters into front and back seats. We enjoyed our day together but were looking forward to another day on the slopes.

The last day we did go out to the slopes. It was sunny but sloppy — wet snow and puddles — one fall and you're soaked. So I decided to follow the old baseball adage: "Wait 'til next year." At age 71, hopefully, conditions will be better.

1997

CHAPTER 14

SAILOR CIRCUS

Everyone loves a circus and the Sailor Circus in Sarasota, Florida is a unique one. Almost all of the performers — over 90 in all — are children, ages 6 to 18; 40 adult volunteers help out. Sarasota was the original home of Ringling Brothers Barnum and Bailey. Many of the Ringling Circus people still live or have retired in the area and help out in putting on the Sailor Circus.

The circus is an extracurricular activity, sponsored by the Sarasota Board of Education, and draws from the many local public schools. The children begin practicing in October and end up putting on ten performances in late March or April. And, let me tell you, they are very exciting and polished performers to watch. It is held in a large tent-like structure and looks like the traditional three-ring circus.

Six months of up to 25 hours of practice a week adds up to a wonderful show for all lucky enough to see one of the sold-out performances. This is more time than the football team spends practicing and ends up with a performance that pleases everyone.

Nancy and I took our five grandchildren and their two mothers to the final show of the year. When you arrive early, you may have the children's faces made-up like clowns. Each of our five had their faces covered with white and then dotted noses, funny mouths and eyes with circles and triangles. This beautiful make-up is done by some of the young performers before they go into their circus acts. Our kids sparkled in their clown-like faces. This got all of us into the festive mood for the show.

The circus band — which plays all night — marched in and set the stage for the 21 acts. The acts were all very good, well performed and fun to watch. Some were really quite extraordinary. We loved the acrobats, jugglers, cyclists, high wire walkers, clowns and tumblers. The first half ended with three young ladies — they looked about 13 or 14 — in a high wire act. Two of the girls walked across the high wire with a bar suspended between their shoulders with the third girl making a pyramid on the bar. No falls and no looks of panic on the performers — only the gaping mouths of the spectators.

The second half climax was an amazing high flying trapeze act. Three girls and two boys flew through the air with graceful leaps, somersaults and catches that took our breaths away. The attempt at a double somersault with a full twist did miss the connection, with the young lady bouncing off the net below, but the overall effect of these gutsy and talented youngsters was a heart-pounding performance.

One of the many scenes at the circus that I shall not soon forget was our three-year-old granddaughter fighting sleep in her mother's arms. It had been a long night for a youngster that age and some crankiness led to a few tears — the paths of which were visible in her clown make-up on her now slumbering face.

The epitome of the sad clown.

1997

CHAPTER 15

FLORIDA ODDITIES

I didn't know that scarlet macaws could roller skate until I went to Sarasota's Jungle Gardens.   John Updike wrote a less-than-positive account of these macaws in his Pulitzer Prize winning novel, "Rabbit at Rest." His characters drive up the Florida Gulf coast and stop at Jungle Gardens. He writes well of the Gardens, but calls the birds "tattered and disgruntled looking."

I have visited the "bird show" at the Gardens several times. The last time was with 100 school children, aged four to ten, who were noisy until the birds came in and began to perform.   The trainer was a young lady, Penny, who seemed to have a close and kind rapport with all the birds.   She said that her "feathered friends live to be 70 to 80 years old but are comparable to two-year-olds with pliers on their legs. They never outgrow the terrible two's." The birds are colorful macaws from Central and South America and the cockatoos from Australia.   They are taught to skate, ride a scooter, paddle a mini-bicycle and drop money in a piggy bank. Frosty, the white cockatoo, at 62-years-old, rides a unicycle on a high wire as he did on Ed Sullivan's television program thirty years ago.   A handsome red and green scarlet macaw balances and walks on a basketball — the only parrot that can do this.   Then he roller skates to the incredulous giggles of the young onlookers.

Penny, the trainer, rewarded the birds for each trick with some birdseed. The children in the audience were excited by the performing birds, and some tried to get close to the stage. They were shooed away by Penny; she related well to the birds but not to the kids. She was protective of her performing friends and didn't want them frightened by the boisterous audience.   Unlike Updike's fictional description of the "tattered birds," I found them bright looking and well taken care of.

After the show, the children could line up to have their pictures taken with one of the birds perched on their outstretched arms.   A wonderful photo opportunity for parents and grandparents, especially with the wide grin but frightened eyes on each bird-holding child.

The sign along the highway said, "Pleasure II. Available Here Hard to Find Valentine Gifts" and "Lingerie Modeling and Sales." I thought, "What the hell — this might be fun." After all, I did own stores that have sold lingerie for 45 years.

I went in and noticed they were renting and selling videos with such titles as, "Fire Down Below," "Huge Grant on the Sunset Strip" and "Foreskin Gump." The "Hard to Find Valentine Gifts" hanging on the wall were soft plastic private parts.

A young lady approached me and asked, "Would you like to see the lingerie show?" I hesitated — found out it was twenty bucks plus tips for the modeling and finally decided, "Let's see."

She said her name was "Arielle," an attractive brunette with long hair, a svelte figure and a rather blank look on her pretty face. I noticed that she had been reading "The Philadelphia Madame." I asked if she was enjoying it. "I like true life stories — just finished Roseanne Barr's book."

I followed her into a small room with a screen, a half-mattress for her performance and a soft, plush easy chair for me "to relax in." Beside the chair was a table with a box of tissues and bottle of oil, both of which Arielle pointed out to me several times. As it turned out, she didn't model, just posed and caressed herself all over. She was dressed in the skimpy but not very revealing outfit she had originally worn. I was continually told to "get comfortable." "You don't look comfortable," she said, making constant eye contact with me as she continued to massage her body parts. I asked how I might get more comfortable. She suggested, "Take off your shoes and work up from there." The idea didn't make me feel comfortable, so I just sat there, gazing at her and jiggling my feet to the rock music in the room.

Arielle said, "For a tip you can see more." I figured, "why not?" and handed her a five spot. She rejected that and said, "The first tip is at least twenty." So twenty it was. She took her "lingerie top" off revealing a tight black bra stretched over a rather flat chest. She kept suggesting I "get more comfortable. I'd like to watch you do it." When I winced, she put her hand over her eyes and promised, "I won't peek."

Arielle elicited another twenty from me so I could see her body-clenching black panties. More rubbing and suggestive looks and finally, after twenty minutes, she said, "We're finished." When I started to get up and leave, she asked me to wait so we could walk out together. "So they don't think you killed me or something." Then for some reason she added, "My sister hooked me on this and I enjoy it. I hope you did."

I was never aroused and we were both disappointed but she had my forty bucks and I had my tale (story).

How did I feel? A little humiliated, a little "taken" and a little better educated on the sex trade in Florida.

1999

CHAPTER 16

TRAVEL TRAUMA

We were visiting relatives in Prague — one of Europe's most dazzling cities. I was taking our niece Rene back to a friend's apartment in the suburbs. The Prague subway system is quite clean and efficient. Unlike the citizens of Prague, I was wearing a N.Y. Mets baseball cap and a leather jacket. I must have stood out as a tourist. The subway door opened, and, as I stepped in, I was surrounded by five people, three men and two women. I could feel their hands all over me. Startled and then angry, I yelled and started to push them away. Shortly, they all disappeared out the open subway door. It was quick, efficient and fortunately non-violent. I was a bit shaken and searched my pockets. Some loose bills in my back pocket were missing, but I could still feel my money belt around my waist. Since that contained most of my stash, I was indeed fortunate. Rene watched all this in speechless horror. As the subway rumbled off, several teenage girls giggled. The rest of the passengers just stared. It was so quick — I couldn't have identified anyone — though I do remember they were short and stocky. It could have been worse. I read recently that Prague still has a problem of theft on the subways and dishonest taxi drivers. I'd certainly go back, but not dressed like a tourist. I'd keep my eyes wide open.

We were touring the Adriatic Coast of Yugoslavia (now Croatia). It was a hot day and going for a swim appealed to us. The three of us, my wife Nancy, friend Nancy and I, walked to the pier to try and get someone to take us by small boat to a swimming area. We contacted one boatman, gestured that we wanted to swim and two of us jumped onto his small craft. He quickly left the dock, leaving friend Nancy stranded on shore. After much frantic motioning, he went back and added Nancy to his boatload. He motored us around the coast until he came to a rocky beach with a large number of children playing in the water and on the shore. As we came ashore, we noticed that none of the children had all of their limbs. Some had one or no arms and/or legs. Others had only one eye or a distorted face. We were, at first, dumbfounded. Obviously, this was an outing for disabled children. We have twelve children between the three of us but had never seen anything like this — forty poor crippled children hobbling about on the pebbles. They were limping, hopping, struggling on old wooden crutches, making the most of their deformities. To our unexpecting shocked eyes it was surreal, heart-rending and heart-warming at the same time. All these limbless children enjoying a day at the beach.

We swam in the cool, clear water near these handicapped youngsters amazed that our boat captain had brought us to this particular beach. Had he intentionally tried to shock us? Or was this beach the best and only swimming area around? He waited while we swam, then sped us back to the pier. Not a word or gesture was exchanged. We did feel good that this poor country was making an effort to give pleasure to their less fortunate children. It was just that to visit them had not been on our itinerary.

We were in Guilin, China, having just gone down the sublimely picturesque Li River, bordered on both sides with strange and beautiful limestone peaks and pillars. Our guide, Lu Hee, was taking us to the Reed Flute Cave filled with illuminated stalagmites and stalactites. She said we would need "fresh rights." We soon figured it out but we had left our "flashlights" back at the hotel.

When we left the caves, which were both fanciful and fun, it was drizzling. The usual Chinese vendors were pushing their wares at us. One young man, hawking umbrellas, was particularly aggressive with my wife. She was wearing a waist pack and he pushed up against her several times. We finally got rid of him and got on our tour bus. Nancy checked her waist pack and noticed her passport was missing — a very serious problem in a foreign country. We went back to the hotel and Lu Hee took Nancy and me by taxi to the local police station. All the police were stern-looking women. We were assured they would "work on our problem." Returning to the hotel, we tried to figure out how we'd get back to Guangzhou without a passport.

At midnight that night we got a call from the police. They had retrieved Nancy's passport and were at the hotel to return it to her. We were thrilled with the quick, efficient police work and wondered what grizzly thing might have happened to the thief. We weren't overly concerned.

1999

CHAPTER 17

VEGAS & BEYOND

Prickly.

I get along well with my six children and their spouses and their offspring. We often vacation together. But with Karen, daughter number two, my relationship is sometimes prickly. Perhaps we're too much alike — opinionated, outspoken, slender. "Dad, you're wrong!" However when I mentioned I'd like to visit Las Vegas and the dazzling new hotels, Karen enthused, "I'll go with you."

Karen lives and works in an ashram, a meditation center. She leads quite an ascetic life, and you wouldn't think it, but she loves to gamble. So we chose a date and a hotel — the new Bellagio — hyped as the finest in the world (or America, or perhaps just Las Vegas).

Vegas is such a hot destination that getting tickets on short notice is difficult. One agent told me, "You can't get there — no seats." To me that was a red flag and a challenge. I ended up going a day earlier than planned and flying to L.A., then back to Nevada. A normal five-hour flight took me twenty hours. It involved kicking a three-year-old blonde out of a seat and onto her mother's lap — and sitting next to a large, balding, serious-looking man in a Promise Keepers tee shirt with his hands folded, as if in prayer. A "Prayer for the Earth" pamphlet stuck out of his pocket.

The Bellagio didn't disappoint. It is classy and gorgeous. If not the finest hotel, certainly the most expensive, built for $1.6 billion, but for a 3000-room mega-casino/hotel, it was eye-pleasing, warm and comfortable. Behind the efficient check-in counter is an original Robert Rauchenberg. The walk from check-in to the elevators passes 2,700 slot machines under orange and red awnings. The elevators, elegant with their mirrors and brass, never kept you waiting more than seven seconds. Quite remarkable for a mammoth, fully booked hotel. The room was comfortably sized and appointed and had a sensuous marble and brass bathroom. The pool area had six different pools in an Italian countryside setting. The gardens were magnificently kept, in glorious fresh shades of pinks. We did like the Bellagio and its small but eye-popping art gallery of top-flight paintings by Renoir, van Gogh, Cezanne and a Rembrandt.

I was unable to stay away from the slots. The dollar machines swallowed my money like hungry bears. A big hairless man near me, however, hit the jackpot. An attendant appeared and peeled off sixty one-hundred dollar bills — 6,000 bucks! I looked at the winner and said, "Wow!" He gave me a dirty look, turned nonchalantly back to his slot machine and cranked in more coins. No sign of elation or satisfaction.

I was alone the first night so I got a ticket to "O," the incredible Cirque du Soleil show at our hotel. "O" was performed on and under water, and each act of this incredibly staged production was breathtaking. Performers dove into the water from crazy angles and incredible heights as if catapulted by slingshots. In their bright and bizarre costumes, they looked like human firecrackers. A piano, played by a lovely musician, glided over the water and then completely disappeared under the waves — forever. The entire performance was a stunner. An expletive ran through my mind with each scene, so I called it "The Holy Shit Show."

Karen arrived excitedly in the room late that night with a bucketful of quarters — 600— that she had just won on the way to our room. The next day, she won another 100 bucks and offered to take me out to dinner at "Le Cirque," a smaller replica of the glamorous New York gourmet dining spot. Even though neither of us had wine or liquor, we were treated well and had a smashing and expensive dinner. Thanks again, Karen.

The next morning I said, "Karen, if we went for a little side trip where would you like to go?" She burst out, "The Grand Canyon." I had already done some research on such an excursion and it topped my list, too.

We flew to the west rim of the Canyon to the Hualapai Indian Reservation. Our first guide was a rotund, talkative man who said he was born in Italy near the Yugoslav border, but then lived in Japan for 48 years. His name sounded like "Bauersnitch." He started talking about Kosovo, said he favored the Serbs, and reminded us of the ethnic cleansing of the Indians. I mentioned that we might have learned that lesson from Hitler. He just grunted. He hated Las Vegas. "Never been to any of those damned hotels." Four non-English-speaking Japanese were in our group and our guide was partial to them. He got them water and snacks, and on the bus ride to the rim, standing next to Karen and me, spoke only in Japanese. He showed them the stem of a local plant used by the Indians for tying. He threw a piece our way and said, "string," the only English word he used on our "instructive" bus ride.

The driver, Norman Honga, was a Hualapai native, dressed in a baseball cap lettered with two-inch-high "NATIVE." He was friendly and helpful and told us a little about his tribe. "There are 1,500 natives here, but the young ones — including my sons — are leaving for West Coast jobs and colleges." At lunch he drew Native American bird symbols on pieces of slate, signed them and gave them to us. Next was the helicopter ride down into the Canyon to the Colorado River. Six of us and the pilot swooped over the edge and flew over a mile, almost straight down, close to the sides of the Canyon. The Japanese ladies squealed and Karen grabbed me tightly. Scary and neat. We landed and walked to the river's edge for a spectacular view, looking up at this most awesome Canyon. Karen meditated and I photographed. She sat on a large rock at the water's edge and communed with the surrounding glory. The reds, browns and grays of the vast walls of rocks, the stark and spiky look of the green and gray desert vegetation, and the steadily moving water of the Colorado transported us — the opposite of all the glitz and glamour and man-made fantasies of the city of Las Vegas. Happy as larks in the bottom of the Canyon, it was soon time to return to civilization. (Civilization? Neither place represented civilization, as we knew it.)

Back in Vegas we moved to the brand new Venetian Hotel — so new it wasn't even finished. No swimming pools, few shops or restaurants open and not many gondoliers. The all-suite rooms were comfortable if a little garish, with lots of Venetian gold and heavy brocade. The outside of the Venetian resembled the Doges Palace with canals and lifeless gondolas. We did spend time in the had-to-be finished casino, which was brighter and more customer-friendly than the other casinos. There were many scantily-clad young ladies eager to get you change or a drink or whatever. Suddenly Karen's luck ran out and the slots sucked up our dollars and then quarters. "Just 20 dollars more of quarters," we kept repeating to each other.

On the way to the airport, I sat with a father and a daughter from Fargo, North Dakota — Scandinavian blonds. The daughter had just turned 21 and her father took her to Las Vegas as a rite of passage. She was shy and soft-spoken and said, "Yes, I had a nice time." Papa said, "We didn't gamble much but we did like some of the free shows."

"How are things in North Dakota?" "It's cold. The population is shrinking. Young people are going to snowless climates." And, no, he didn't like the movie "Fargo." "That's Minnesota."

Las Vegas is filled with huge, punchy signs. The last one I saw before we left had a telephone number and said, "VASECTOMY REVERSED." I didn't jot down the number.

Karen and I had a wonderful time — excitement and laughter and sighs. In a large family it is a joy to be one-on-one with a loving relative. Being with Karen and the sparkle of Las Vegas made me feel young and alive. Karen said, "Dad, you've got more energy than I've seen in ages." Karen — you're the elixir.

The prickliness had disappeared.

1999

CHAPTER 18

PHOTOGRAPHING THE NUDE I

While visiting friends in East Hampton, my wife, Nancy, showed me a notice in the local paper about a summer course in photography at nearby Southampton College. As a retired retailer and amateur photographer, I was interested and called and signed up. It so happened that the first week's course was "Photographing the Nude" with master photographer Ralph Gibson.

I went to Southampton College on Monday for the first lesson as per the prospectus. Gibson didn't show up.

There were twelve enrollees in the course. Six were young Japanese students — five of whom spoke little or no English. The other six were local people — three adults and three college-aged students.

The next day Gibson arrived. He thought the course started on Tuesday. He offered no apology and took us to a house in the Hamptons complete with lovely pool and gardens. There were three female models and they reminded me of the story of "Goldilocks and the Three Bears." One was a little bit heavy, another a wee bit old and the third one was "just right." We were to take turns photographing each model by the pool and around the gardens. Most of us wanted to photograph Tina, "Miss Just Right." After the first day, we never saw the older model again.

Tina told us stories of working with a famous French photographer who took her to California. She soon split up with him, "because he insisted I sleep with him and I refused." (Tina seemed to be making a play for Gibson, I imagine to further her career.) The other model, the slightly plump Laura, was a pleasant local young lady who also worked as a gardener.

After the initial sensation of seeing the nudes, I found it was not very different from photographing flowers or statues, except we did have to pose the models. At first, Gibson gave the directions for the poses and then we were asked to do it. When it was my turn, I had the two models pose in the garden picking flowers. Gibson said, "That was weak, Swezey." My rejoinder was, "Grandchildren are a lot easier." (It is unusual to tell indifferent naked strangers what to do.) Gibson proceeded to have them pose in more exotic, but not erotic, positions.

One day we went to a waterfront house on Shelter Island with an attractive swimming pool. It was a hot day; we took lots of pictures and swam in the pool. At one point, I asked the one Japanese student who spoke English if he had this much fun in Japan. He smiled and said, "not legally." Evidently, in Japan it is illegal to photograph or show pictures of pubic hair.

Gibson had been drinking beer and was in a good mood. He had Tina placed up in a tree about six feet off the ground and arranged her in a Jane-like shot. Then he decided to get in the picture himself. He stood about a foot in front of the tree with the nude Tina over his head. The resulting shot had Gibson in the foreground and Tina high in the background — which I guess was his intention.

On the final day Gibson showed slides of his own master photographs. Many of them were truly exciting. He also gave a brief lecture. He was both arrogant and bored. I had never seen anyone lecture and yawn at the same time. He looked at our work and gave suggestions and criticisms — some helpful.

To quote from his lecture gems: "If you learn how to photograph the nude, you can photograph anything." "It's a metaphor for all photography." "To photograph the nude, you have to have an idea." He quoted the famous Robert Capa, "If your picture didn't turn out, you were too far away."

To improve our work Gibson suggested we take at least seven rolls of pictures a week. He said it used to take him five to ten rolls to get a good picture. Now he gets good ones in every roll. We asked if he would show us his work for that week so that we could compare it with ours. (He had pushed us aside if he thought he saw a shot he wanted to take.) Gibson said we would see his work in book form in a year or so.

Finally he was asked to give us a grade for the course. "Give 'em all a B," he said. I got an A.

What did we learn? Take lots of pictures and get closer to the subject, especially nudes.

1996

CHAPTER 19

PHOTOGRAPHING THE NUDE II

Well, not exactly.

I had signed up for a workshop in photography in Cortona, Italy, an Etruscan hill town in Southern Tuscany. The course was called "Robert Farber, The Nude," and featured Farber, a noted photographer of un- or barely-clothed people. It was a two-week course with Farber and the nude models coming the second week. I wanted to stay away from home for no more than a week, so I registered for the first week only — a shoot in the town and surrounding countryside. No nudes were scheduled. My interest is in family and travel photography, so I had no need for nudes.

I flew to Florence and stopped for a short while in Lucca, a walled town with medieval buildings. It was the home of Giacomo Puccini of "Madame Butterfly" fame. However, it was not until I got to Southern Tuscany and the Cortona area that I became truly excited about the landscape and photo-beckoning hill towns.

It was spring and the green of the early crops, yellow of the fields of rape, and red of the prolific poppies on the rolling hills dotted with ancient sienna-colored farm houses were overwhelming.

The ride south was exciting, but in a different way. There is no apparent speed limit on the major Italian highways. This certainly grabs and holds your attention. I would cruise along at 80 m.p.h. and "whoom," a BMW or Mercedes would pass me as if I were stalled. One silver BMW passed me like a rocket. It was doing at least 200 m.p.h.! This can be nerve-wracking when you are not used to it, especially when you feel the need to get in the passing lane yourself. And, when cars approach you from the rear, they all seem to want to see what's in your back seat. No driver in Italy seems to have heard of the dangers of tailgating.

Why are they all in such a hurry and why is it that all the German cars — BMW, Mercedes, Audi, Volkswagen — must pass you quickly and immediately? Are they all rushing to get out of Italy? Every couple of miles along the highway is an SOS sign and telephone. I can understand why, although I never did see an accident.

Driving on the back roads is more relaxing, except for the hairpin turns, but no one seems to drive leisurely enough to enjoy the view and the pace becomes catching. I remember one set of hairpin turns where the car behind would honk me around each turn. I was still taking them on four wheels. The male Italian driver appears to be a frustrated race car driver who must think it is against the

49

law to put a foot on the brakes. Highway courtesy is not a priority in Italy — although one driver did honk and gesture as I was about to back off a precipice.

When I finally arrived in Cortona, my first hotel room was higher than it was wide and when claustrophobia set in I asked — demanded — to be changed to the adjacent room which I could see was twice as big and comfortable.

The Cortona Center of Photography is run by two photographers from Atlanta, Georgia, Allen Mathews and Laura Fellows. I soon found out this was their first workshop in Italy. They had only six participants and they were struggling to make their efforts into a success.

Laura, a fortyish brunette, had gone to photography school but became bored and decided to try out as a photographer's assistant. She met Allen, they clicked and have been working and living together for the past 14 years. Laura is warm and friendly and looks like Debra Winger (not quite the star quality). Allen is a handsome, white-haired 60 — very low-key and quiet. He had worked in advertising photography, i.e., the Coca-Cola account, and I was very impressed with the black and white work he showed us, mostly Cortonese people and scenes. I bought a couple of his prints.

Laura and Allen put their life savings into getting this venture off the ground and had an impressive list of famous photographers coming to lead workshops throughout the next six months. Their success so far was borderline.

The other five workshop members were all professionals in the field of photography and had outstanding work to show, and were certainly on a different level than my point-and-shoot amateurism. They all had expensive manual cameras and talked a different photo language than I did. However, after the initial hesitancies and ego-strutting, we got along well and I was accepted for what I was — a retiree with a hobby — and, I like to think, a pretty good eye for a shot. Allen said to me, "You're doing fine. Don't change a thing." The others were not as generous but they had their own agendas.

My own favorite photo-mate was Jeannie, and we went on several shoots together as we had similar interests. She was a black and white photographer from Delaware and had taught her craft and shown her work in local galleries. I thought her work was absolutely superb — landscapes and people that burst from the page. I told her I had to have some of her prints — she sells them for $300 to $400 and I think they are worth every cent. We worked out a special business arrangement for several.

Jeannie was quiet a first and seldom spoke about herself. I said to her, "Jeannie, you're one of the few people I've met whose favorite topic is not themselves." After we got better acquainted she confided that she had just gone through a divorce. She said, "My ex-husband is a fine man — I still love him very much." This made me regret my initial remark.

Her camera equipment was all top-notch, including a 4 X 5 view camera. We enjoyed walking through ruins, old farm houses, planted gardens — she was a part-time farmer — and bright poppy fields, photographing together.

Jeannie was a most compassionate person. She was helpful and concerned about Laura and Allen, and wanted to stay and work with them in Cortona. She went out of her way to befriend Robert, a young man in our group who seemed to be having social and legal problems, and drank a bit too much. Her caring seemed to be a big boost for him. She could see that I was out of my element with the others and was kind and considerate toward me. I was impressed with both her talent and her humanity. She was a most enthusiastic and passionate photographer. She would rave about each sight we found and shoot in the glorious Tuscan countryside. Robert, the young man from Miami, Florida, appeared to be fighting demons. He did not always show up for a shooting session but, thanks to Jeannie, seemed to level off as the week went on.

Jim, Jay and Dave were all from New York City and chatted on about cameras, techniques and developing processes. Dave, whom we called "The Rabbi," was a young Jewish man on a Kosher diet. He had a degree from Yale in ancient Near-Eastern studies and spoke five languages, including Italian. At first I thought he was a phony and show-off, but he calmed down and became an interesting, helpful and warm-hearted addition. He was anxious to shoot models, especially nudes, and had taken several such workshops from top photographers. His work was eye-popping, including his nudes, and some rather unusual travel photographs of Stockholm, Copenhagen and Iceland.

I was anxious to bring my wife back to this wonderful Tuscany area and hoped she would be enthusiastic about doing so. Thus, one night, I decided to splurge and go to the four-star restaurant/hotel just down the hill from Cortona — Il Falconniere. It is in a small farming area with sweeping views of the valley below. It is an exquisite, small hotel, only twelve rooms, spacious and beautifully decorated in the yellow and orange colors of Tuscany.

The owners are a handsome, late-30's, Italian couple. Silvia, is a lively blonde — one of the loveliest women I had ever met — a young Julie Christie, and equally charming. When I went in to dinner and stopped for a drink in the couched bar area, Silvia and her husband were there and I showed them some pictures of my stay in Cortona (from the 1 Hour Photo store). He was indifferent but she was very gracious. An older, balding, goateed man came into the room and was introduced as "the best photographer in Italy." He was Gianni Renna, whose specialty was food and interiors for "Grand Gourmet of Italy." He was doing a picture layout of Il Falconniere. Needless to say, my pictures were never mentioned and he never looked my way. A copy of "Grand Gourmet" was passed around. It had a striking plate of food on the cover so I asked if Sr. Renna had photographed it. "He didn't do that one."

Silvia sat with me on the couch (loveseat size) and we chatted amiably. I thought, "My God, she is the most beautiful woman I have ever sat this close to." Her English is choppy (my Italian is chopped) and we ended up discussing the difference between "hungry" and "angry," both of which she pronounced "ongry."

Soon I went into the brick, vaulted-ceilinged, dining area with soft yellow and navy accents — a most elegant room. I ordered the prix fixe dinner under the heading "Silvia Suggests." I found it disappointing. The lamb was a bit tough and the dessert — a caramel sauce on strawberry sherbet(?). However, six other Americans who ate there all raved about the food. I must have, as usual, ordered wrong. I think I was overwhelmed by Silvia and her suggestion. I certainly do plan to return to this very special inn on the hill when Nancy is with me.

As I checked out of the inn the next morning, I asked Silvia, who was working on her computer, if I could take her picture. She said, "Okay," and bounded out into the sunlight to stand by her rosebush. "I don't photograph very good," was her comment. I thought, "Yeah, like Julia Roberts." When I finished, she said, "I hope your machine is still going now." Yes, my machine is still going now and the picture turned out to be quite a prize.

Cortona I found delightful — full of friendly people, some of whom I got to know in my week's stay — a local artist (another Silvia, who painted intriguing abstract acrylics), a woodcarver, the photo store man, waiters at the outdoor café, and Elizabeth, the linen vendor. The village has virtually no crime (I was told) and everyone seemed honest and forthright, in contrast to the Italy I remember fifty years ago when everyone appeared to short-change me. I did have a problem with the local woodcarver. He overcharged me and then was most apologetic when I brought it to his attention. I was later told by a fan of Cortona that it was "an honest mistake."

The streets of Cortona are narrow and steep. Vehicle traffic is discouraged, except for deliveries and luggage to the hotels. I needed to bring luggage to my hotel after my night at Il Falconniere. On my way up, I sideswiped a parked truck on the already tight street and then needed a place to park. A lady police officer was on duty and, by hand signals and my limited Italian, she understood my short-term parking need and directed me park far down another width-deprived street. We both agreed on five minutes. I delivered my luggage and had a quick cup of tea with some photo friends — seven or eight minutes. When I returned to my car, I saw a wide truck stuck behind me and the driver standing in the street in Italian agitation, hands and mouth moving. Near him was the lady cop, writing me a ticket. I gestured I had been given five minutes but to no avail. After complaining to anyone who could speak English, I misplaced the ticket. Now I am awaiting an overseas summons and bill.

At first, Laura, our leader, brought in local young ladies, fully dressed, for portrait shots. One, Silvia #3, the flower seller, had almond-shaped eyes and a twinkling smile. Another, Elizabeth, was a shy but beautiful brunette who sold Florentine linens. They were both fun models to shoot but the pressure was on to get to the nudes. On my last day there, Laura brought a professional model and part-time actress (spaghetti western) from Rome. And guess what? Her name was Silvia. She had a wonderful body, radiant skin and an expressive face. She seemed to satisfy everyone. We shot this Silvia in a windowed room in Cortona with ancient walls just outside as a background. Then we lunched on the steps of the Court House. I had my picture taken sitting next to Silvia #4, licking a gelato cone and smiling broadly.

That afternoon we went out into the countryside to an old farm house owned by friends of Laura. There Silvia posed in the buff standing in decaying doorways and against battered-looking stone walls. She also posed on a white couch in a rather neglected second floor room.

I had bought, from Silvia #3, a fresh bouquet of flowers for our model, Silvia #4, to hold and had her pose topless but wearing an attractive brown print sarong around her waist. Then, of course, I took a few full frontal shots. The others, except Robert, wanted nothing between their lens and Silvia's flesh.

Robert had the final shoot with Silvia and he had her remade up with dark make-up around her eyes. Then he wrapped her in bubble plastic and had her stand on the back of a bright green, three-wheeled, Italian pickup truck parked in the farm yard. She held up an 8-inch crystal ball and posed like a wicked but battered statue. Silvia was not thrilled with all this, so Laura whispered to Robert to try some flattery. He spoke nicely to her and she responded with an exotic pose. I'm not sure what Robert's aim was but it became a most unusual shot, and we all, except Silvia, got a big kick out of it.

There were three young girls, aged six to ten, in the farm yard, running around, climbing trees, sprinkling each other with the hose and otherwise having a grand time. Since they were the ages of my granddaughters and each had an inviting face, I took more pictures of them than of the professional model. The ten-year-old was a budding artist and posed with some paintings we all admired.

I had a most satisfying and memorable week of taking pictures. I can't wait to return with Nancy. Tuscany is extremely shoot-worthy, but it was the people and the people pictures that made the trip — four Silvias, et al. — even (and especially) with their clothes on.

As I left, I gave each photo friend a stamped postcard with my address on it to send me a report of "photographing the nude with Robert Farber."

Some replies:

"Women, women, all naked. Jay."

"All models and no landscapes. Where are you? We miss you. L. Jeannie."

53

"We got bush today again. See you soon. Oh, look for my pics in 'Hustler's' Beaver Hunt. Ciao, Robert."

"Robert Farber was a very good instructor — models all very shapely. Dave."

"What a finale — beautiful models, great weather, everything turning green, beauty abounds. Amore, Laura and Allen."

No word from the four Silvias.

2000

CHAPTER 20

THE EXHIBIT

I'm not an artist. And there I was, lined up for a photograph with two artists for a "Meet the Artist" session at the Community Building in Sayville.

I had been asked to show my photos of New York City by BAFFA (Bay Area Friends of Fine Art). I mounted twenty pictures of the Big Apple. I was moderately pleased with them. They weren't too exciting but not really embarrassing either. My last photo exhibit, at a local library, was about South Africa and had been quite well received. Everyone seems to like wild animal pictures, especially lions and leopards up close.

For the BAFFA exhibit I was paired in a room with a professional photographer, Sylvan. He does computer-enhanced shots of flowers that he has grown. The results look as if they were done in watercolors and are quite startling. People who came to our exhibit hovered about his photos and then glanced at mine. I watched one man yawn as he looked at my first pictures and gave the balance the millisecond treatment.

The second artist was Fabian, a young man of Ecuadorian origin, who painted Latin American countryside scenes. I especially admired one of his colorful village paintings, with the Andes in the background, and asked him the price. "Sorry, that's the one of this group that's sold. To a doctor."

When we were asked to pose for a picture of the "artists" we made an interesting contrast. Sylvan is a dark African-American and wore a black casual jacket, red sport shirt and a black bandana on his head. Fabian is a short, swarthy, tousled-haired young man in a white open-necked sport shirt. I am a balding, older man with glasses, shirt and tie. There we were - An African-American, an Hispanic and a Wasp. The problem was that two were real artists and I'm a retiree who takes pictures.

As I left I heard two young men talking. One said, "I like the New York style." I thought he was talking about my pictures. It turned out he was discussing pastrami sandwiches.

TWO WEEKS LATER - The picture and a write-up of the three of us appeared in the local paper. "The final artist was Kim Swezey, a retired retailer. Mr. Swezey has been taking photographs for fifty years and this current showing of scenes from New York City shows that he has developed a fine eye for detail and composition."

I'm glad the reporter looked.

I was pleased.

2000

CHAPTER 21

VIENNA

How could I resist the offer of going to Vienna with the American Ballet Theatre? I'm mad about ballet in general and the American Ballet Theatre in particular. The trip itinerary sounded irresistible. Our guide, an Austrian countess, would take us to palaces, castles, museums, artists' studios, three ballets and an opera. I did have some misgivings: I'd been to Vienna when my daughter spent a semester there. It is a picturesque city with a great musical heritage, but some of the people were, well, feisty — at best. It was a city that initially received Hitler with great enthusiasm. Also, my wife, Nancy, and ballet friends couldn't go, so I would be going alone. I was afraid the rest of the group would be snobs from the New York City social scene. Nancy urged me on, so good sense prevailed and I went to Vienna with twenty stately ballerinas and assorted others.

The group turned out to be congenial. It included a young and glamorous New York City doctor, a couple from Santa Barbara, California, who were friends of a relative of mine, and a couple who I learned later had just given a five-million-dollar gift to the American Ballet Theatre.

Our guide, the Countess Calice, was a down-to-earth, but very well-connected and beautifully dressed Viennese woman who had worked in New York at the United Nations with Kurt Waldheim, the controversial Secretary General of the U.N. When I asked her about him, she said he had made mistakes and had a mammoth ego, but was a competent and honorable man.

The countess showed us an exciting time. Our opening dinner at the Palais Pallavicini was a sumptuous affair held in the Imperial apartments of the Hofburg Palace Complex, built by the Hapsburgs. The gilt-edged room had high ceilings, Baroque stucco designs, and the grand mirror effects of opposite-mirrored walls. The dinner, featuring veal Orloff and finishing with old Viennese Shankerlcremebombe, an elaborate coconut sundae, was served to us at a long table lit with ornate candelabra and brilliant sconces on the palace walls. Our hosts were the Markgraf Pallavicini and the Prince of Liechtenstein. Both were tall, portly men of advanced years. I asked the Prince if he skied, and he said, "I'm too busy now." The ladies in our group were all dressed most elegantly. Our lovely doctor was wearing a smashing, short-skirted, bright silver and gold tailored outfit that really made the Prince sit up and take notice.

I went to the ballet four times — three times to the American Ballet Theatre performances and once to the Vienna Ballet performed in the Vienna State Opera House, with a guest performer, Vladimir Malakov, a member of the American

Ballet Theatre via Moscow. He is a striking dancer with wonderful leaps and as soft a landing as I've ever seen in a dancer — like a leaf floating to the ground. However, the rest of the cast of the Vienna Ballet were not up to the standards of the American Ballet Theatre performers.

The American Ballet Theatre danced in what had been the old stables of the Hofburg Palace, an adequate stage but it was not the Metropolitan Opera House or the Vienna State Opera. The first performance featured three of their most fetching ballerinas — Julie Kent, Susan Jaffe, and the sensational young Paloma Herrera.

Ms. Kent is an enchanting dancer, and I felt that she stole the show with her wonderfully graceful dancing from the ever-popular pas de deux from "Swan Lake." "The New York Times" recently called her "ethereal." I was sitting in the center of the front row, six feet from the stage. It was as if Ms. Kent and her partner, Jeremy Collins, were dancing for me in the privacy of my own room. What a treat!

After the performance, we met some of the dancers at an informal reception. I met and was photographed with Paloma Herrera. She is perhaps the most exciting young dancer today. Her teenage interest in talking to a senior citizen was brief at best. As I tried to chat amiably with her, her eyes darted past me to the handsome young Cuban dancer José Carreño. Then she strode away in that duck-toed yet graceful walk that all classical dancers seem to have.

The following day we again visited the Hofburg Palace, the winter palace of the Hapsburgs, and saw the magnificent court tableware and silver. After, we went into the countryside to visit the Alt Erlaa Castle, home of Baron and Baroness Loudon, descendants of General Loudon, who had been Marie Theresa's counselor and whose statue we had seen at the Hofburg.

Baroness Loudon is a very attractive lady with two teen-aged sons. Her radiant face was tanned from a recent ski trip in the Austrian Alps and was accented by her golden blonde hair. She was a friend of the Countess and made us all feel how happy she was to have us visit Vienna and come to her home. She was an absolutely charming and warm-hearted hostess in her gracious country house. The tables were filled with goodies for our eating pleasure.

That evening we went to a private reception at the Baroque Vienna Museum of Fine Art, hosted by Mrs. Ferrero-Waldner, Austrian State Secretary for Foreign Affairs. The museum is a magnificent building with lavish interiors of dark marble, polished wood and massive statues. The art collection includes works by Rembrandt, Vermeer, Caravaggio and Velázquez.

Some of the dancers were there and I was asked by an American Ballet Theatre hostess which dancer I'd like to meet. Who else but Julie Kent? Julie was very friendly and we had a wonderful chat. Julie is 26, younger than any of my five daughters, and has been dancing for ten years with the American Ballet

Theatre. She is most attractive — blonde, slim and radiant with a high-pitched voice and the enthusiasm of a young girl.

She said, "Look at my ring. I've just become engaged to Victor Barbee (a fellow dancer)." She was bubbling over as she showed me her dazzling diamond. As the two of us were chatting, television lights and cameras were coming toward us to interview her. At the same moment, someone else came over to say I had to leave to go to that evening's performance. Julie was not dancing that night, so I bid her adieu, telling her I thought she had been the star of the first night. I just missed my chance to be on Austrian TV.

The next day we were to go down to Melk in the Wachau Valley. I had been there before, so I decided to stay in Vienna and see Julie dance the matinee's performance. She danced the Tchaikovsky Pas De Deux with Jeremy Collins. I was thrilled all over again. She was incandescent in her strong but delicate leaps and impeccable line.

Vienna is a city of intriguing history. We visited Freud's studio, well preserved from his day. The guide told us that Mahler, one of the many musical geniuses who lived in Vienna, was a patient of Freud's. However, Freud did very little for him because he didn't want to interfere with any of Mahler's creative genius. I can hear them now.

Mahler:	"Sig, my hands sweat and shake when I compose."
Freud:	"That's bad?"
Mahler:	"It's distressing."
Freud:	"I can help but it might poof your creativity."
Mahler:	"I'll sweat and shake."

We also saw one of Mozart's studios, but it was disappointing. It had what seemed to be Swedish modern furniture, a few period posters and earphones to listen to "The Marriage of Figaro." I've never associated Mozart with blond modern furniture, but his music is sublime.

The area around the historic Saint Stephen's Cathedral was filled with shops, galleries and lots of strollers. The people were conservatively dressed and stared at the white sneakers I was wearing, and when I spit down the grate in the gutter, I shocked the passersby. I thought I might be arrested, however most Viennese were friendly and no one seemed feisty this time.

On the plane trip home, I sat among the returning dancers. I was intrigued to see lots of pairs of feet in the air. Apparently this was to stretch and keep limber. I didn't try it.

Ballerinas, Julie, Paloma, Vienna, Mozart, Freud, The Countess — a most tantalizing trip.

1996

CHAPTER 22

BALLET

In the last ten years I have developed a passion for the ballet. I had always been interested in the arts, but had never seen much ballet. I remember going to a retrospective of the wonderful English sculptor Henry Moore at the Metropolitan Museum of Art. I was much impressed with his soft, graceful lines and strong body statements. That evening, I went to see the New York City Ballet perform Balanchine's "Symphony in Two Movements." It was sublime. I remember thinking that the lines, forms, shapes and sculpting of Balanchine's ballet affect me much more than Henry Moore's sculpture. From then on I was hooked.

The recent spring ballet season in New York City was absolutely outstanding. The American Ballet Theatre's "Romeo and Juliet" with Alexsandra Ferri and Julio Bocca was a heart-stopper even though I'd seen them dance it several times before. Ms. Ferri dances as if she has no bones in her body and is a superb actress. Mr. Bocca is a virtuosic dancer and a wonderful complement to Ms. Ferri with his high leaps, soft landings and tender partnering. This season, Mr. Bocca also danced with Paloma Herrera — a sensational, young, teenaged ballerina who was superb with a youthful exuberance in her first starring role in "Don Quixote."

Aside from the Balanchine's repertoire, the New York City Ballet also has a world-class roster of dancers. I was enchanted by the two Darcies dancing the leads in "A Midsummer Night's Dream," Balanchine's witty and wonderful adaptation of Shakespeare. Darcy Kistler, the wife of the New York City Ballet director Peter Martin, and their showcase dancer, has such a radiant presence as a ballerina. Darcy Russell, a great dancer this season from Britain's Royal Ballet, is one of the all-round loveliest creatures the world has today. She has an innocence, sensuality and exceptionally pretty-girl-next-door look to go with her technically brilliant dancing. Balanchine would have been proud of this cast — Ms. Kistler was the last ballerina he crowned for stardom before his death. I was certainly overwhelmed.

Then there is Pilobolus. This Dartmouth-originated group of six dancers combines modern dance and acrobatics to give us passion, humor, and dashing and exciting movement. Adam Battlestein does a hilarious solo dance with five cylinders and a chair. Rebecca Jung and John Sevilla did an almost nude dance starting off as two blobs and ending up as two human lovers — very exotic and beautiful. Finally, all seven do "Rejoice," a ramble through "Finnegan's Wake" that is witty, sentimental and a wonder.

I can't wait for the next ballet season — the fun of going into the City with friends, having delicious dinners at different restaurants near the dance theaters and then seeing the grace, beauty and elegance of the world's finest dancers.

1998

CHAPTER 23

DANCING WITH THE DANCERS

A chance to dance with the dancers of the New York City Ballet was more than I could resist. I persuaded my wife Nancy, sister Pris and brother-in-law Jerry to go with me to the benefit dinner and dance.

We wondered "would the dancers show up and stay more than ten minutes (it was their only night off) and would they dance with us?" "What was funky black tie and were we dressed appropriately?" "Can we still waltz?" (They waltz a lot on stage.) "Who else would be dancing with the dancers?"

We arrived at 8:00 p.m. and watched the "guests" slowly assemble outside the New York State Theater and then meander in — young — very young, slender — very slender and most attractive. And in all manner of dress. The young women (the women were all young) wore very short dresses showing their lovely figures or even shorter dresses with lacy see-through dresses over them. The men — all black —all white — from formal to tee shirt. What we wore didn't matter. It was not the usual ballet crowd.

We walked up to the second floor where we saw many attractively decorated tables — white and black with candles — and a small dance floor in the middle. Champagne, wine and booze flowed freely. Our table was in the corner at the end of the buffet line. We were told six strangers were to sit at our table for ten. One or two jackets had been left on chairs, but when the young guests saw our group at the table, they picked up their jackets and smilingly walked away, afraid of the ageing virus, I guess.

Undeterred we went out on the balcony and chatted briefly with some of the dancers we recognized. Then to the buffet which was catered by Sylvia's of Harlem — yams, collard greens and fried chicken. Well, we hadn't come for the food. We noticed some of the dancers milling around, some dressed conservatively and others standing out: Melinda Roy in a very colorful hat and pants outfit she had designed herself; Bob LaFosse in all black with a black beret; Yvonne Bouree in a striking long red dress; Albert Evans in a shiny red jacket, short shorts and long black boots; and Jack Soto in shiny black leather slacks, black and white tee shirt, and a large silver belt buckle — a New Mexican American Indian dressed as a Fire Island cowboy.

Soon the music started. It was all hard disco music played by 14 guest DJ's from Nicole Miller to David Salle.

Darci Kistler and Peter Martin led the way and soon the dance floor was throbbing with young dancers and the New York disco crowd — and the four of us. It was quite a scene with all kinds of dancing from sedate cheek-to-cheek to what looked like intercourse on the dance floor (the groin grind). At one point, someone grabbed Darci Kistler and danced wildly with her until a fellow dancer rescued her. I could see why most of the ballet dancers preferred dancing with their compatriots.

It was hot dancing on the crowded floor, so some of us went out on the balcony. It was hot out there, too. The scene there was of an older man seated on the balcony rail with his young pretty partner dressed in a very short canary yellow dress standing nestled between his open legs — each with itchy hands and moist lips. And in a corner was a couple so closely embraced that there was no space at all between them.

A return to the dance floor — and the eager, young women with their escorts of varied ages with a few ballet dancers mixed in — brought us more exciting disco stepping.

Over half of the principal dancers of the New York City Ballet did not show up. It has been a long and grueling spring season with over 70 different ballets danced — the most ever.

Fortunately, I had a camera to record some of the action. As the only naturally bald-headed man there, would I go again? You betcha!

1995

CHAPTER 24

DIAN

Dianne, Diane, Dian. Three "Dianes" have touched my life.

Dianne Leone was the executive secretary in our store when I was president. She was smart, dedicated, attractive and a joy to work with. Dianne was promoted to store manager of our third branch and has recently returned to manage our largest store. She was an immeasurable help to me and still is, and I'm very fond of her.

Diane Darling was the minister of our Congregational Church for four years. She was the first openly gay minister of any Congregational Church in America. Diane was a warm person, a dynamic preacher, and attracted many new members to our church, especially lesbian women. Her time in our church was not without controversy and she left quite abruptly to return to the West Coast. I liked Diane and was proud of our church for calling her and supporting her for four years.

And then there was Dian Fossey, a most intriguing person. I never met her but I have been fascinated by her life. She was a legend in her time and died a tragic death. I have read four books about her and seen two videos.[1]

Dian was chosen by Dr. Louis Leakey to do research on the mountain gorillas of Central Africa. She spent more than 18 years in a passionate and determined effort to document the gorillas and ultimately befriend and help save them.

Dian had been trained as a physical therapist and spent ten years with retarded and autistic children. After reading George Schaller's work on the gorilla and hearing Dr. Leakey speak on the subject of the great apes, she became obsessed with wanting to work with gorillas. Under Leakey's guidance she went to Africa and in 1967 established a research camp, which she called Karisoke, in

---

[1] Books: Walking With The Great Apes by Sy Montgomery

Gorillas in the Mist by Dian Fossey

Woman in the Mists by Farley Mowatt

Land of a Thousand Hills by Rosamund Carr

Videos: National Geographic: Search for the Great Apes

Gorillas In the Mist

the Virunga Mountains of Rwanda. She was totally committed to her work and, in spite of occasional bouts of poor health and several returns to the States, spent almost 20 years studying the gorillas.

Dian was a six-foot, dark-haired, brown-eyed, handsome woman. In the "National Geographic" video of her work she was soft-voiced (not what she was known for) and looked startlingly like my own mother as a young woman. Her work focused on the habits and plight of the gorillas, which were being attacked by poachers and pushed around the jungle by Hutu farmers who needed more land and Tutsi herdsmen with large flocks of cattle.

Mountain gorillas grow up to six-feet tall and can weigh over 400 pounds. They are the largest and most feared of all the great apes. Dian's research showed them to be shy, gentle and non-aggressive vegetarians, who would attack only if directly threatened.

After several years of observing Dian was able to approach them and interact with them. The "National Geographic" video shows her exchanging food, touching and patting and being playful with these giant apes. It is astounding to see her in contact with her huge friends in the wild. She became especially close to a gorilla she called Digit, a silverback male. When Digit heard Dian in the distance he would scamper from his group to greet her. They would sit together and playfully enjoy each other's company.

During her years of work in Rwanda Dian documented the habits and features of over 90 different gorillas. She became obsessed with her new animal friends. Her relationship with the gorillas almost always took precedence over her relations with humans. She said, "I feel more comfortable with gorillas than people. I can anticipate what a gorilla's going to do, and they're purely motivated." However she had a lusty sex drive and initiated short-lived affairs with a number of men.

Dian took time off to lecture in America and teach at Cornell. After teaching for a semester in Ithaca she was voted the favorite professor on the campus.

Back in Rwanda the poaching problem became worse. A number of gorillas, including Digit, were killed. Dian was beside herself and continued to violently pursue the poachers and even burn their camps, all without the cooperation of the Rwandan authorities that she sought.

Many research students came to Karisoke to help in the gorilla study. Her relations with the students was often tenuous. Dian put them on anti-poaching duty. Her focus was entirely on the gorillas, not the needs and interests of the students. One student was Kelly Stewart, a Stanford graduate and the daughter of actor Jimmy Stewart. She was bright and dedicated, without a trace of Hollywood in her. Kelly and Dian got along well at first, but Kelly's too-close friendship with Sandy, a fellow male researcher, put a strain on Dian's tolerance.

Kelly is shown working with Dian in the "National Geographic" video. We see Kelly encountering her first gorilla. However, when Kelly became enamored with Sandy and later married him, she was turned off by some of Dian's violent anti-poacher antics. They worked together for several years but Kelly's assessment of Dian after her death was negative. "Dian was no good as a scientific worker, but still she couldn't hand over control. She couldn't take the back seat. She viewed herself as this warrior fighting an enemy that was out to get her." Not a very generous postmortem.

A true friend of Dian's was Rosamund Carr, an American who had settled in Rwanda, and worked as a farmer and inn-keeper. Now in her 80's, she still lives in Rwanda and runs an orphanage to help some of the children of the genocide of the mid 90's. Rosamund befriended Dian and often took care of her when she was ill or needed help. It took a while for Rosamund to get beyond Dian's gorilla-obsession, but she writes, "Ultimately I came to love her and admire her very much, but it was never an easy friendship. Dian was absolute in many things. But beneath her brash exterior there was a soft, feminine side to Dian which many people never knew. She loved to shop and she loved beautiful clothes. Dian and I argued frequently about people versus animals, and I believe that there were many things about Rwanda that she didn't understand. There is no doubt, however, that it was Dian's dogged determination and sometimes controversial methods that rescued the mountain gorillas of Rwanda from almost certain extinction."

Dian, with her volatile personality, tunnel vision toward the gorillas and against the poachers, and her heated arguments with Rwandan authorities, made many enemies. She knew she was in some danger.

One night an intruder entered her cabin and split her skull with a *panga.* This brutal murder was never solved to the satisfaction of the American officials. A Rwandan court convicted, in absentia, an American researcher who had been working with Dian at the time. Most people outside of Rwanda still believe that the killing was related to the poacher problem.

Rosamund Carr, at 73, made the two-hour mountainous trek to Karisoke to attend Dian's funeral. Dian was buried in the grave site where she herself had buried her beloved gorillas — including Digit.

Dian's death focused the world's attention on the plight of the mountain gorillas and helped stabilize their existence, at least until the horrifying genocidal war in that most unfortunate country.

I shall probably never see gorillas in the wild but I shan't soon forget the valiant effort of Dian Fossey to save them.

POSTSCRIPT

The latest word that I've been able to get from Rwanda is that both sides in the dreadful war now realize the importance of the gorillas to their country. It appears that the gorillas are protected while thousands of Africans are slaughtered. Thus Dian's legacy of concern for these great apes, hopefully, lives on.

1997

CHAPTER 25

MARYLIN AND BOB

Funeral parlors are a tough gig. How do you best express your sympathy? What do you say except "I'm sorry — we're thinking of you."?

I especially remember the visit to the family of Marylin Reza. We knew the Rezas socially. Bob Reza was my wife's doctor, and he and I were on the hospital board together.

Marylin had been brutally murdered. The story, as reconstructed at the time, was that someone had broken into the Reza's home, gone upstairs, discovered Marylin in bed, and shot and killed her.

What can you say to a husband at the funeral parlor at a time like that?

We got to the parlor early, and Nancy and I were one of the first ones to talk to the family, Bob and his two teenaged daughters. I expressed my sympathy to Bob. He looked me deep in the eyes and said, "Kim, never forget to lock your house up. There are weird people out there." He seemed in control of himself, though his daughters were quieter and naturally very tearful. I was impressed with Bob's courage and composure.

Nancy and I left and on the way out in the hallway we met and spoke to a friend who was a homicide detective on the local police force. He said they had no solid leads but were working hard on the case.

Bob Reza was a large man with dark hair, dark skin and bushy eyebrows. He had full lips and a confident manner. He looked like a friendly gorilla.

His family came from Mexico, but he was born and educated in this country. He became a doctor specializing in lung and respiratory diseases. Bob was extremely bright and well respected, and was on the faculty of the nearby university hospital. His father was a minister and Bob was very active in his local church.

Marylin was an attractive, petite woman with porcelain skin. She came from the midwest, had trained as a nurse and worked in Bob's office. She, too, was interested in the workings and teachings of their church. They both taught Sunday school and she sang in the choir. As a family, they tithed and she fasted and prayed one day a week in respect for her family and church. Marylin was a most thoughtful and caring person who didn't appear to have an enemy in the world —or even anyone who ever spoke in anything but the most glowing terms about her.

And then came the bombshell! About a week later, Bob was indicted for the murder of his wife. Nancy and I and all their friends were completely shocked! Not the good Dr. Bob. They had seemed to be so close — an apparently idyllic marriage. In any murder, the spouse is always a prime suspect, but it didn't seem to make any sense at all in this case. The Rezas worked together and prayed together, enjoyed similar interests and appeared to be a very close-knit family.

What could possibly be behind this? Lust or greed? Sex or money? As it turned out the organist in the Reza's church told police that she was having an affair with Bob. She had moved out of her home to live with her mother, leaving her husband and three children. The organist's father had been a good friend and patient of Bob's, and when the father was dying of cancer several years before, he asked Bob to take care of his family.

Bob Reza dictated a twelve-page confession to the Suffolk County Police. He began:

> "Shortly after Thanksgiving, 1990, I was so frustrated with my life and I decided to buy a gun and decided to kill my wife, Marylin. I have never been able to cope with success. I have brought this upon myself. Marylin was my real half. I was the technician. I targeted Marylin because it was the beginning of the end for me. I could never kill myself. I knew by killing Marylin I would be caught and I would go to jail and wither away and die."

He went on to detail how he did it. He had gone to a medical convention in Washington, flew back unexpectedly, committed the murder and returned to Washington. After he shot Marylin, he took his necktie and strangled her — just to make sure. In the confession, he never mentioned his affair with the organist.

During the ensuing trial, Reza pleaded not guilty by reason of insanity. He said he had snapped from guilt over extramarital affairs (apparently numerous), job pressures and his role as an elder in his church.

Reza's two daughters, who stood by him, begged the judge for leniency. One girl said, "What sort of justice is it that will take my last parent away from me?"

The judge, quoted from the Bible, "To whom much is given much is expected." He then sentenced Reza to 25 years to life in prison.

The following holiday season during a sermon talkback at our church (not the Rezas'), the question of Christian forgiveness came up. I thought of Bob Reza. I did not feel I could forgive him. I certainly did not and still don't understand his motive, but I decided that as a human being reaching out to another I would write him a letter. I mentioned what was going on at the hospital, spoke of his children with whom my wife had been in contact, and just made it a chatty, informal letter.

Bob wrote back from Attica where he had evidently been transferred from Wende Correctional Facility. He said, "I had a little trouble with the Wende C.F. It is now all in the past and I am doing reasonably well here at Attica." He told of getting a job as a tutor in the Consortium College. He wrote of his daughters, who had visited him recently and seemed to be doing well.

He ended up:

"Again thanks for the kindness of writing. I hope you and yours have a lovely Lent and Spring Season. Warmest Regards, Bob."

Recently I heard from a reliable source that Bob Reza had remarried while in prison.

So much for withering away.

1996

CHAPTER 26

ALFRED

I have had several friends and a father commit suicide, and I've always felt I might have done more to prevent these deaths.

Alfred and I were in the same class in high school and became close friends. He had a good sense of humor and was fun to be with. Neither of us was very athletic; he was a pretty good student and I was near the top of the class. We both came from quite well-to-do families — each father had a substantial business in the area — and we were both headed to college. We both seemed to like the same girls — however, it was often that a third boy ended up getting the girl. Alfred's father worked hard to keep him out of the draft but I was most anxious to enlist. He went into the Merchant Marine and I went into the U.S. Army Infantry.

Neither of us saw combat; we went on to college and both eventually married and settled within ten miles of each other in our respective family businesses. Al married a local girl I had dated, though not seriously, and I married Nancy, my sister's college roommate. He and his wife Polly raised boxer dogs, while Nancy and I raised six children, plus dogs, cats, birds, gerbils and rabbits. Except at Rotary meetings or an occasional cocktail party, we seldom saw each other and drifted apart.

We did have some business associations — he a roofer and I a retailer — not a particularly friendly or lasting relationship. At my bidding his company had done a roofing job on one of our retail buildings and our landlord was very unhappy with his work.

Al had very few friends in our area, maybe one, and I bumped into this friend, Bill. Although Bill was a friend, he did not have much good to say about him. "Al is a taker, not a giver." Bill said that Al and Polly drank a lot. Polly had had a blood clot and had fallen out of bed, and Al was too drunk to help. She subsequently died. I missed the funeral, not being aware of what happened, but I did call Al to express my sympathy. He was retired and heading for his condo in Sarasota, Florida — coincidentally, the same city where we had a small house. He was planning to leave soon and I said I'd call when we got down there.

Al and I met several times in Florida and went out for dinners and concerts. He would have a couple of drinks but seemed to be able to hold his liquor.

Al missed his wife and talked quite a lot about her. He had a few friends in Florida, but when he returned to Long Island, he seemed alone and lonely. I decided to visit him at least once a week to see if I could help. He had lost his sense of humor and had few interests — watching golf on TV and eating and drinking.

We went out to different restaurants in our area and out toward the Hamptons. I always drove. He didn't know what to do with all his money. His father had been a founder of our hospital and I was on the board, so I suggested a memorial gift in his father's name. That didn't get very far because he was upset he'd never been put on the board. Actually he really didn't deserve to be.

Al's drinking increased. I became more concerned and went to the minister who had buried his wife. The minister promised to see him and try to help, but was not optimistic about an alcoholic. He never did contact Al. I continued to see Al weekly when I was home and finally told him I'd have to stop if he didn't ease up on the bottle. He would sometimes be so drunk when I picked him up he would stumble to the car.

After I spoke to him he was slightly better. Then I went out of town for a week. On my return I had a funny feeling about Al and drove to his house. There was no answer at the door so I walked in and found him in a drunken stupor, sprawled on the bathroom floor and mumbling about pallbearers. I called the police.

An ambulance took him to the hospital. Aside from the drinking he had been an incessant smoker and his body was in very bad shape. Within a few days he was dead. Al had lost the will and motivation to live, so he, in essence, drank himself to death.

His sister, with whom he had little or no contact, (they had feuded over his father's estate) came to the funeral as did a few scattered Rotarians who knew him.

What could I have done? Insist that he go to A.A.? Take him out more often? Get him to a doctor?

I did try to help, but I failed.

1995

71

CHAPTER 27

EULOGY FOR A FRIEND

John White and I were very close friends. We had a special relationship. He lived two houses away and we lunched together several times a week. Although we didn't always agree on some of the minor topics of life - sex, politics and religion - we got along extremely well, thanks in part to his warm sense of humor.

I can hear him now. "Swezey, sit down and be quiet." But he was kidding me and didn't mean it. We teased each other continuously and that was a part of our friendship. Two days before he died I asked him about all the women coming to his hospital room to kiss him. Even then he teased me back.

When I think of John, which is often, I think of him as a man of great integrity, courage and compassion - and a family man par excellence.

His integrity was beyond question. He was a great credit to the legal profession. He made all those lawyer jokes seem like complete and total lies.

He had the courage to stand up for what he believed in. John blew the whistle on the local establishment about things he thought were wrong and, for a while, this hurt him in the community. But he stood by his guns.

And his compassion for his family, friends and community was legendary. John helped start Brookhaven Memorial Hospital over forty years ago. He was its first secretary and later served six years as president of the Hospital Board. He probably spent more time and effort on our hospital than anyone else.

He doted on his family - his wife "Jeannie" and his three wonderful daughters, Susan, Jeanette and Rosemary and he was, of course, proud of all his grandchildren. His secretary Jo Ann became like a member of his family.

John was quite a man, honest, courageous and loving to his family and friends, with a big heart that he used for good constantly until it finally wore out.

John, we'll miss you immensely and will remember you with much admiration and love.

1999

CHAPTER 28

WARREN

Our family knew Warren Buffett when he was plain old Warren, an eccentric but brilliant investor and long before he was "The Second Richest Man in the World." My brother-in-law, Jerry, got to know Warren through his own brother, Tom, who went to Columbia Business School with him.

Susie and Warren Buffett and their three children would frequently come to West Meadow Beach on Long Island to see Tom and Jerry and spend a few weeks. Warren never went out on the beach. He stayed in the beach house and read the steady stream of newspapers and articles that was delivered to him. He would play bridge at night in a quiet, serious way, but he had a sense of humor about the game and teased his beaten opponents. I showed him a magazine piece about the shellfish industry. I was interested in the people involved, some local people, but Warren concentrated on the business potential. "Too much reliance on the forces of nature."

His wife, Susie, dark-haired, lively and pretty, took the children around to the local sites on the South Shore. But Warren never budged. Their children and our children — ages 6 to 14 — played "War" in the beach grass and swam and clammed together.

Warren had an opinion about children and money. He felt that spoiling children was a cardinal sin, that giving or leaving them a lot of money would lead to disaster. He called inherited money "food stamps for the rich." Recently he said, "The kids have gotten modest gifts right along but they're not going to live the life of the super rich. I think they probably feel good about how they've been brought up. They all function well and they are all independent, in that they don't feel obliged to kowtow to me in any way." This attitude became a strong, confirming influence on Priscilla and Jerry and Nancy and me.

Pris and Jerry went out to dinner with the Buffetts, and Warren said, "Pris, you pick out the restaurant." She chose a French bistro. Warren looked at the menu, got up and asked the waiter if he had a good steak. Even then, steak and Coke were his favorite foods. After dinner, Warren pulled out his American Express card and paid for dinner. When Priscilla later admonished Jerry for not offering to pay, Jerry said, "Come on, Pris. He owns American Express."

Warren told Jerry he wanted to learn to play the ukelele. Jerry knew how and wrote out detailed instructions for learning the instrument and sent them to Warren. In return, Warren found out Jerry was coaching a Little League baseball team and sent Jerry baseballs autographed by the Hall of Fame pitcher Bob Gibson for each team member.

Jerry contracted leukemia and lay dying in a New York hospital. I thought about contacting Warren so he could telephone Jerry — but I never got around to it. I'm sure he would have called and Jerry would have been thrilled. To this day I regret my omission.

When Jerry died, Warren sent a five-page, handwritten letter to Priscilla telling her what Jerry's friendship had meant to him. He ended by saying, "I'm only a phone call away. Please don't hesitate to call for any reason."

For many years we went to the annual meeting of Berkshire Hathaway. We would sit in the front row of the Joplin Museum auditorium and could ask Warren questions from the floor. One time I asked about the contrast between value and growth stocks. Warren is known as a value investor. He replied, "Not much difference. If a company has great potential for growth, it's a good value."

After one meeting, I wrote him a letter with some suggestions about the over-crowded meeting place. I also threw in a stock suggestion. Warren sent me my letter back with four sentences penciled in the margin about handling future meetings. He does not like outside stock tips and never mentioned my proffered suggestion. But he had saved money on stationery and a secretary, and does (or did) have the reputation as a penny-pincher. When he broke down and bought a small corporate jet for his company, Berkshire Hathaway, he called it "THE INDEFENSIBLE." When he began to use it constantly flying to New York to help rescue Salomon Bros., he changed the name to "THE SEMI-INDEFENSIBLE."

Since Warren has become such a celebrity, perhaps the biggest in the money world, we've stopped going to the Omaha meetings. Too many people — there were 15,000 at the last meeting and they lined up at 4:30 a.m. to get in. And too much hoopla. Warren is shameless in promoting his portfolio's products — Coca-Cola, Sees Candy, Dairy Queen, Borsheim's Jewelry, Nebraska Furniture Mart, GEICO Insurance, etc. But, we will admire him. And buy his portfolio products.

One of my favorite Buffett quotes, which I think about almost daily, is "Stock Market forecasts tell more about the forecaster than the future." So much baloney is written and spoken every day about which way the market is headed that it is most helpful to keep Warren's words in mind.

Warren on wealth: "Money, to some extent, sometimes lets you be in more interesting environments. But it can't change how many people love you or how healthy you are."

We love you, Warren. Stay healthy.

1999

74

CHAPTER 29

KRABLOONIK

Crash! Bang! Ouch! "Nancy are you alright?" We had been thrown out of our vehicle. Our vehicle was a dog sled, pulled by thirteen dogs with a musher in the back. The snow was icy and slippery and, as we went around a sharp, steep curve at a good speed, Nancy and I were thrown out into a deep snow bank.

We had been skiing in Colorado for several days and had rarely fallen on the slopes. But this dog sled fall hurt. Bruised ribs and the wind knocked out. However, no broken bones, so we gingerly got up and walked haltingly down the hill to try and catch up with the errant sled.

After our tumble we caught up with the dogs and sled about a half mile down the trail, and got back on to continue our trip. The driver was apologetic but not overly concerned when he saw we weren't seriously hurt. The rest of the ride was slower and more relaxed, but our ribs began to ache.

We went through the trees and into the woods and stopped in a snowy meadow to give the dogs a rest and to stretch our stiff, sore legs. We were offered a cup of wine or hot chocolate — whatever. Then the leisurely trip back to the kennels.

The owner of Krabloonik is Dan MacEachen. Each year he enters his dog teams in several races including the famous Alaska Iditarod over 1000 miles long.

This year, 2000, he entered the International Mountain Stage Stop Sled Dog Race (IMSSSDR). This race is held in Wyoming and is a qualifying race for the Iditarod. MacEachen's team finished fifth in a field of 23 and he felt he could have done better. He had to put a dog in the sled four different times to avoid further injury and bloating which he says "can result in lethal injuries if the dog doesn't rest." For sledding the injured dog, MacEachen was awarded a sportsmanship medal, the first time given, "for deep concern for his dog's welfare." "They're family to me," MacEachen says. "I have a very good idea of what they can do and taking them beyond that breaks the trust they have in me."

The sled dogs are from Krabloonik, one of the largest sled dog kennels in America. They have over 250 dogs including a continual parade of recently-born puppies. The dogs are hybrids of original sled dog types — Malamute, Eskimo and Siberian — all commonly known as Huskies. These dogs are bred just to work on sled dog teams and are not for show or sale. However, Huskies do make good pets, since they are even-tempered, affectionate and intelligent. For a good sized monetary consideration you can go on a two-hour dog sled ride, bundled up in furry coats supplied by the kennel. The driver or musher stands on the back of the sled and directs the lead dog and the others with verbal commands, no whip or rein. The lead dog is not necessarily the strongest or biggest or most intelligent but, according to the musher, is "an instinctively born leader."

MacEachen runs the popular restaurant at Krabloonik associated with the kennels to help pay for the care and training of his several hundred dogs. It serves unusual game meats — caribou, elk, wild boar and pheasant plus salmon and trout. We took our grandchildren there for a tasty lunch. They liked the elk burgers, but their favorite part of the outing was visiting the kennels and petting and holding the Husky puppies. We took some joy-filled photos of Liz, young Nancy, Annie and Kimmie holding these warm, fuzzy, affectionate animals.

MacEachen says Krabloonik means "big eyebrows" which is an Eskimo term for "white man." In our family Krabloonik means excitement, good food and, to the grandchildren, soft, snuggly dogs.

1999

CHAPTER 30

TWO LARGE PIZZAS

My brother-in-law Jerry had been given two wild ducks, recently shot. They were hanging by his back door as we arrived at his house. My sister, Priscilla, and my wife, Nancy, decided to cook them. Between the plucking and the gutting and the cooking they gave up in disgust and said, "Why don't we send out for pizzas?"

A friend of mine recently told me of the wonderful pizzas he had eaten from "The Homestead" or some such local joint.

I called "The Homestead" and said I'd like two large pizzas. The man on the phone said, "Where are you?" I replied, "I'm in Blue Point and I'll be over in twenty minutes." "OK."

Jerry and I arrived at "The Homestead," an old Victorian house just off Main Street. There was a "Homestead" sign out front but nothing about pizzas. We knocked on the front door and told the man we were from Blue Point to pick up two large pizzas. He invited us in.

Down the front stairs came two young ladies, moderately attractive with wry business-like smiles. No pizzas in sight. Jerry and I looked at each other with stunned expressions on our faces, mumbled something about pizzas and left in haste.

Outside we noticed a rose-colored piece of glass above the door with a light behind it.

We jumped in the car, doubled over in laughter and drove away. It was then that I realized it was the "Hometown" pizzeria I had been told about —not the "Homestead."

When we got back to Jerry's house Nancy said, "What took you so long?"

1997

CHAPTER 31

TOPSFIELD FAIR

"I loved the pig races." "Riding an elephant was cool." The joy and fun of the Topsfield Fair was enthusiastically enjoyed by our family — two grandparents, one mother and five grandchildren — all girls 5, 8, 10, 11 and 13.

Founded in 1818, the Topsfield Fair in northern Massachusetts is the oldest continually-running fair in America. It covers 83 acres and features numerous buildings of agricultural displays and shows. The day we visited the fair, over 100,000 people came through the turnstiles. We were fortunate (foresighted) enough to arrive as the fair opened and had several hours before the big crunch made moving about and enjoying the sights difficult.

The first attraction we saw was an ageing Asian elephant, Beulah, slowly walking around a small track with children on her back. Our five girls quickly got in line and together had a short but eye-popping ride on top of Beaulah. Later Trish, our 13-year-old and an avid animal lover and sympathizer, said, "The elephant was old and feeble. She should be retired."

The nearby petting zoo tent featured antelopes, an oryx, a yak from Tibet and, the center of attraction, a 14-foot Masai giraffe. For a quarter, we bought some pellets to feed the giraffe. He bent his long neck down and slobbered on our hands. More fun.

A real highlight was the pig racing. Four of the Robinson's Racing Pigs ran at 15 m.p.h, around a short track to win an Oreo cookie. We sat on abbreviated bleachers and cheered them on. Each of these smallish, pink-skinned pigs is numbered and we bet among ourselves. The winner got a bumper sticker that said, "I love Robinson's Racing Pigs!" The pigs were all named — "Dolly Partham," "Hilary Rodham Clintham," etc. H.R.C. won. There were two races and we all got laughs and thrills from this unusual event.

Nearby was the pig barn. There was a long line to get in but the children thought it was worth it to see the pig pens of lovable baby pigs, some suckling up to their mothers.

Another barn had guinea pigs and a multitude of different and odd-looking rabbits. Our eight year-old Annie was looking to buy a guinea pig. The guinea pig in her school classroom had died and she wanted to spend her allowance to replace it. She met the man selling guinea pigs and, after listening to his lecture on their care and feeding, she bought one. This really made Annie's day and her generosity and happiness warmed all our hearts.

We were impressed by the care and kindness of the guinea pig salesman, the sheep-shearing lady and others whom we encountered at the fair. Although it soon became crowded with long lines and shoulder-to-shoulder masses, everyone at the fair was polite and considerate.

Our next stop, the poultry barn, was intriguing — the noise, the 1,000 prize chickens and the large heated box of hatching eggs. Our grandchildren were fascinated to see the egg crack and then watch the scrawny baby chick stick its head out and finally stumble away from its birthplace with bits of shell still hanging on its back.

An egg judging contest awarded prizes based on color, size and texture — the prizes — $3 for 1st, $2 for 2nd and a buck for 3rd. Not a get-rich-quick possibility.

Several religious organizations were represented at the fair. The local Congregational Church had a large tent where they served home-cooked meals. The line there was too long for us, so we settled for hot dogs and ice cream. A Fundamentalist Church was housed in a small building with a video and computerized quiz. Kim, our youngest, was quite taken with the video. "We got to listen to what God said."

I was taken by the computerized quiz. One multiple choice question was: "Do you believe in a God?" Possible answers were:

    A. "Yes, the Bible says so.
    B. "Nobody knows for sure."
    C. "No, it's just made up."
    D. "We hope so."

On most questions, I kept looking for "none of the above." I guess in their eyes, I got it wrong. Each answer was supported by a quote from the Bible. As we left, we were all handed a small copy of the New Testament. Kim had a happy smile on her face.

We drifted over to the amusement area with rides of thrill and games of chance. Kim and I were attracted to a ball throwing booth with a sign that said, "Everyone wins something." The object was to throw a ball and have it land in a red cup — 90% of the cups were white. Five throws for $2. No one was throwing at this booth, so the carny lady kept handing Kim balls to throw — 25 in all until (a) a crowd came over to watch and/or (b) she got it in a red cup. Both happened and Kim was given a very nice stuffed dog that she clutched to her side for the rest of the day. Well worth the two bucks.

Two of the grandchildren, Liz and Nancy, 10 and 11, are inseparable cousins. They are also tops in their respective classes in looks and brains (a grandfather talking). They agreed that the scary rides in the amusement area were the best of all. The adults liked the pig races. A wonderful family outing at a lively country fair.

1998

CHAPTER 32

VLADIMIR AND MIRASLAV

"It was a dream!" Those were Miraslav's last words as he left from Newark to fly back to his native Prague after three weeks in America.

"It is a waste of 42 years to live under those horrible Communists." He spat out the word Communist. Those were some of Miraslav's first words to us as we arrived in Prague — three years earlier — our first meeting with him.

Miraslav is the brother of my sister-in-law Dana's late husband Vladimir. Vladimir was a Czech citizen who worked for the French underground in the 50's and helped smuggle Czech citizens from Prague to Paris. At one point, he was caught by the Communists but escaped by swimming across an ice-cold river and struggled over the mountains — eventually reaching Paris again.

Vladimir married a wealthy American in Paris and had one child. His wife was killed in an auto accident. He then came to America and met Dana, Nancy's sister, in a bar in Boston. They married and had four children.

Vladimir was a man of adventure. Before the Communists came to Czechoslovakia he had been conscripted by the German army. He escaped forced labor and made his way back to Prague where he hid out with his mother and brother until the end of WWII.

In America his (and my) father-in-law, Don Hunt, set him up in the travel business. As a sideline he learned to fly and ferried single-engine planes for Piper all over the world, even Australia. Here, too, he had several mishaps but always seemed to land on his feet.

Vlad was a lean, wiry man who kept himself in top shape by constant exercise and careful diet. He resembled the ballet dancer Mikhail Baryshinikov. He had a certain charm and was an interesting man with his wartime experiences and world travel. We became good friends. He and Dana flew to Sayville to visit us one weekend and on the way back the plane crashed on take off. Dana was pregnant at the time but was hurt only slightly. Vlad had multiple fractures and spent several months in our local hospital. Nancy and I visited him every day. He eventually recovered and went back to work as a travel agent.

Vlad talked about his mother and brother in Prague. At one point he heard that his mother was being allowed to visit relatives in Germany. He flew to Germany to see her. She was so terrified of the consequences — she had been followed, threatened, and told never to see him — that she hardly spoke a word to him. Vladimir was heart-broken.

Then he made a fatal mistake. He went on a travel agents' familiarization trip to Moscow. Vlad later told us he was followed everywhere and an attempt was made to compromise him with an attractive young NKVD agent.

On the way back from Moscow his Aeroflot plane was diverted to Prague. He anticipated what might happen and scribbled notes to several nearby passengers. Czech police boarded the plane and took him to jail. He was tried as a traitor — his own brother was forced to testify against him — and sentenced to life in prison. He was kept in a cold cell, beaten and almost starved, but he tried to maintain self-discipline and keep his body and mind in shape.

Our mutual father-in-law, Don Hunt, worked day and night to try and free him. Vlad had become an American citizen so our government was involved. It was a long slow process. The State Department and Senator Ted Kennedy worked on it for months. After about a year and a half he was released. Rumor had it that there had been financial considerations including a $30 million dollar ransom.

Vlad's return home was joyous but the joy didn't last. He never was the same after his prison experience.

He drank, battered Dana and took off for Fort Lauderdale where he passed out on LSD. Though I had written to him in jail, he hardly spoke to me again, except to say that my letters were dull.

Within the year he moved to Spain and several months later his body was found at the base of a mountain. His death remains a mystery: Speculation - suicide.

My father-in-law told me that just before he died Vladimir sent him a letter thanking him for all he had done for him and apologizing for the trouble he had caused the family. Don said that in spite of the problems he and Vlad always got along well.

Ten years after his death two of Vlad's children decided to visit their uncle in Prague. They were received royally and loved the city. Their experiences encouraged Nancy and me to make the trip. Uncle Miraslav and his close friend Jarina met us at the airport and carried our luggage on the subway and bus, taking us to our hotel.

Miraslav is much different from his brother Vladimir. Before the Second World War he had been a concert pianist and performed throughout Europe. After Vladimir's exploits in the French underground became known, Miraslav was arrested by the Communists and forced to work in a uranium mine for over ten years. After he was freed the puppet Czech government assigned him the job of train conductor for five years. Eventually he was allowed to return to his conservatory to teach and accompany singers. He still does this today.

Almost six feet tall and slightly chubby with a ruddy complexion and warm smile, Miraslav is affectionate to his friends and relatives but his true passion is music and Prague. His health suffered from the years in the uranium mine but he never complains and has plenty of energy.

Miraslav talks of the 42 years of his wasted life under the Communists. But, he did say he doesn't hold it against Vladimir that he and his mother suffered so much extra agony at the hands of the occupiers because of his brother. When he was told of the $30 million ransom he put his hands on his forehead, reddened and was almost incoherent.

Miraslav and Jarina spent a week lovingly and proudly showing us their beautiful city of Prague — which had not been damaged by the war. We went to the opera, ballet and many historic sights.

Jarina is a calm, stately, handsome older woman who had been both dancer and singer and was still giving singing lessons and concerts. Her late husband had been a noted Czech folk artist and illustrator, some of whose work is in America. Her English is better than Miraslav's so she helped all of us by occasionally translating. They have a remarkable and close relationship — the major bond being music.

One of the highlights of our trip was a visit to Jarina's modest but attractive apartment with pictures on the wall of her, nude or dancing, painted by her husband. We were served wonderful plum dumplings, a Czech delicacy. After lunch, with some urging, they gave us a concert, Miraslav playing and Jarina singing — Moravian folk songs and Czech classical music. He encored with a George Gershwin medley. Nancy and I applauded with enthusiasm.

We discussed them coming to America and two years later they arrived. Miraslav was overwhelmed and ate up every minute of his time in New York. Jarina had been here before but was still thrilled.

We took them to the Metropolitan Opera four times. His excitement was boundless. He lit up like a kid at Christmas. "Le Elixir D' Amour" is a gay, colorful, melodic, funny, beautifully-staged opera and was sung by young singers Bonney and Alagna and Met veteran Paul Plishka. Our Czech friends loved every moment. The Met's lavish and sumptuous production of "La Traviata," beautifully sung, brought tears to Miraslav's eyes.

Miraslav has a great interest in singers and conductors. His knowledge is extensive; his likes and dislikes are very strong. He is enthusiastic for Battle, Domingo and Upshaw, the conductor Fuertwinger and the old records of Farrar and Caruso. He dislikes Waltrous Meier. "She's German, typical, strong, Wagnerian, <u>not</u> a Carmen." And he is exacting about the facts of the singers and opera. When Jarina said "Barbara Bonney is 35," he replied sharply, "No, she's 33."

After a week with us in New York, they travelled to Massachusetts to visit Vladimir's family, wife Dana, the four children and his ninety-five-year-old father-in-law, Don. The trip was emotional and overwhelming. The children and Don were dazzled by Uncle Miraslav, and he was tender and loving with them.

A week in Florida at our vacation house in Sarasota followed. They walked the beach during the day and listened to Mozart CD's at night. He had difficulty using our showers and no interest in our washer or dryer or dishwasher. Nothing mechanical — everything by hand. However, they both loved our refrigerator. Jarina had one that was over 25 years old. "I'll have to get a new one." And the same for the toaster and vacuum cleaner.

Everything was compared. "In our country" was a constant phrase. They enjoyed their rest and relaxation in Florida, but after three weeks were ready to return to their beloved Prague.

Both brothers have brought interest and stimulation to our lives. Nancy and I talk about them frequently. Vladimir was charming and exciting but his daring led to tragedy.

Miraslav added a new dimension for us. He is an inspirational man — after 42 years of deprivation he has become a man of hope and enthusiasm and good cheer. He is a highly cultured new friend with a richness we look forward to enjoying again and again.

1997

CHAPTER 33

IT'S MAGIC

I have wonderful grandchildren, five girls - ages three to eleven. They exceed my fondest expectations for children of that age, but we often don't have the same interests. I wanted to bridge that gap. Thus, I decided to become a magician. I could do it for them and with them, and we'd all be entertained.

The magic store had lots of tricks and I chose what I thought would be easy for me and fun for them — newspapers that hold water, balloons that don't burst when punctured, light bulbs that turn on in your mouth, cards with numbers that change easily. The hottest new trick in the world of magic — a dollar bill dancing in thin air.

I practiced and became modestly proficient. The girls enjoyed the tricks and then I would teach them.

One day, my daughter-in-law, Beth, asked me to put on a little show for Trish's birthday party. I prepared well and dressed in top hat and black jacket, and the show seemed to go quite well. The next day, I got a call from Beth who said a mother had asked her who the wonderful magician was that her daughter was talking about and was he available for hire. Beth laughed and said, "That was just my father-in-law."

I did another show for my granddaughters and their friends at a beach party. A young lady there — a neighbor — was five-years-old and too much for me. She knew every trick and would announce to all how it was done. On other occasions, some children would yell out "I see it, I see it" and reveal my magic (not my grandchildren, of course).

Finally, I rehearsed with five children — including nieces and nephews — ages three to twelve — and we put on a show at a Rotary Christmas party. Each child would do his or her magic, and then I would perform. That day everything seemed to go wrong — my balloon burst; my water leaked from the newspaper. Even the dollar bill wouldn't dance. Finally the Rotarians yelled, "Come on, Kim, let the kids do the magic — you sit down."

The kids loved it, but I stopped performing until I could collect my ego and talents.

The grandchildren and nieces and nephews still enjoy getting new tricks on their birthdays and we still do magic together — but seldom with a demanding audience.

1996

CHAPTER 34

RETIREMENT AND BUSINESS

I worked for forty years in the family department store — half of that as its president. The store was started 103 years ago by my grandfather.

When my father graduated from Harvard Business School, he decided he didn't want to be a retailer and he worked on Wall Street. The business was sold and went downhill. Eventually my father decided to buy it back and put it on its feet.

My father was a kind, generous, creative, thoughtful, hustling man, a good father and a thorough gentleman. He worked very hard reinvigorating the business and the store did turn around. However, after a number of years, he had a nervous breakdown. He never fully recovered and I have nothing but the fondest memories of him. He died in the 60's and I feel great sadness for the suffering caused by his health problems. My mother stepped in to help run the store.

My mother was a tall, beautiful woman with lots of energy and talent, and a very caring attitude toward all who came in contact with her. She was loved by family, friends and fellow workers and became an outstanding role-model for my five daughters. She lived to be 93, active and interested to the very end.

After 13 years of schooling and a stint in a New York City store, I entered the family business. We had a wonderful staff, opened two branches and were a successful and profitable store through the 80's.

After reflecting on my father's history and forty years of my own involvement, I decided that running the store was no longer enjoyable. The stress was affecting my marriage. The next generation — my son, John, my sister, Priscilla, and her sons, Dave and Bill — were able to carry on, and I had saved and invested enough to retire.

Thus, I quit active participation, became Chairman of the Board, and relinquished all day-to-day responsibilities. What a relief! Now I could experience the joys of retirement. I did have the luxury of having a desk at the office but my time was completely my own.

Our family's business philosophy is that nothing will come in the way of family solidarity: We would sell the business before it would hurt or divide the family. Despite numerous bumpy roads, that philosophy still works today. Much of that success is due to the caring and generosity of my sister and her two sons and John.

I write memos and make suggestions and my relationship with the fourth generation is very good. However I have been told recently by my son that I am not quite on the cutting edge of retailing today (half-jokingly, of course). Personnel and merchandising were my forte and occasionally, I'll be asked for an opinion on a touchy personnel problem but never on merchandising.

At one point it was decided to have monthly stockholder meetings. As a stockholder and non-working Chairman of the Board, I was invited.

For this meeting I decided to write a report on the new branch — the third — that has never quite gotten off the ground, doing about half of what our demographic survey had projected.

I spent time in that branch and community and talked at length with our bright, capable store manager, Dianne.

I came up with a list of suggestions for improving sales in the store. One was to have harder hitting ads with a bigger store logo so our name would stand out. I measured the logo of the competitions' ads (Macy's, Sterns, Lord & Taylor) and, although we were the least-known store, our logo was the smallest.

I put all my ideas together in report form, went to a local Kinko Copy Center and got fancy folders and colored copies made so it would have more punch.

I had been told that my memos were read as avidly as Warren Buffett's annual reports (our family members are all Buffett fans and investors — lucky us!) I handed out the reports at the meeting, although I was not too hopeful my ideas would be taken seriously. There were many other pressing problems.

At first no one said much about the report except our new comptroller — formerly an accountant — who seemed enthusiastic. However, he was new to working in retailing and was not yet a full-fledged merchant. Nothing was said over the next couple of weeks either, however Dianne did seem aware of some of my ideas.

Then one day I opened the local paper, noticed our ad and took a second look. I got out my tape measure and, sure enough, our logo <u>was</u> bigger and more in line with our competition. I could hardly believe it!

The next day I saw my son and my nephew and asked if our logo had really increased in size. John, my son, said, "Yes, but it hurt sales because it took space away from another item we wanted to put in." He was kidding (I hope) and he laughed.

So I feel I am not completely out to pasture and may even continue to occasionally use my retail brain to try to help this 107-year-old family business prosper in the future.

1997

CHAPTER 35

SWEZEY'S - ONE HUNDRED YEARS LATER

It really is a milestone in retailing to have a family business thrive through four generations - 100 years.

I was told a number of times that the competition might be too much for us. First it was the Bee Hive in its modern new store down the street. Then it was Korvettes - the first of the discounters. Then the big malls opened, Walt Whitman and Smithhaven, featuring Macy's and A&S. Then more discounters - Mid Island and Jeffries. All these stores are now either out of business in Chapter 11 or closing stores but Swezey's is looking ahead.

A recent issue of "The New York Times" carried an article on the resurgence of the traditional department store which was given up for lost several years ago. However, now the feeling is the future is brightening - because the department stores keep putting out strong advertising and treating their customers better. A story in the "Wall Street Journal" tells of the problems facing the so-called outlet centers. They're trading up and not giving the customers the bargains they expect.

The discounters are still popping up but aren't we all discounters? About three quarters of all we sold at Christmas was at a discount. So the customer benefits and retailing goes on.

The key to retailing is people. These are a few of the people I remember in Swezey's first 100 years. My grandfather, A.M. Swezey (Arthur), was the founder. He was at the end of his career when I came to work for the store. I remember that he always had candy in his pockets for the customers' children. He was a super salesman. Among other things he sold fur coats. I went with him to a customers's home when he was selling a coat. His technique was overwhelming; she could not resist. And A.M. had time for the community - he was mayor of Patchogue from 1928 to 1930.

My father, Carroll, was the consummate gentleman and also the most outstanding merchant I ever knew. He wanted every department to "sizzle" with best sellers and he made sure they did! He was an excellent teacher to Jack, Pris and me.

My father's health was not strong and at one point, my mother came in and had to run the store. She was one of the famous "Henrietta's" * in Suffolk County. She seemed to know everyone who came in the store, and had a kind and caring word for all. She was also ahead of her time in women's rights and their place in business and the community. She was elected to the school board and was told by the other members, all men, that she could help pick out the colors for the new school. This bit of sexism got her dander up and my mother became a strong force for good education in our town. She was a wonderful role model for all the women (and men) in our family and in the store family.

Our V.P. Jack Luchsinger was the best sales promotion person I ever knew. I remember fondly the promotions to Hawaii, Italy, Switzerland, Mexico, etc. He was a man of strong character and a pillar of the community. He was an excellent teacher to Marilyn, who took over after he retired and has continued to do a an outstanding job.

My sister, Priscilla, has been called the "heart of the store." She is a fine merchandiser, and shows a genuine and caring concern for all who work with us and for our customers as well. She has lived during four generations in the store and it looks like she'll never retire until the fifth generation is firmly in place.

We are most fortunate with our fourth generation - John, Bill and David. It is unusual and lucky for us that they are all deeply interested and capable of leading Sweezey's — in certainly one of the most difficult economic periods on Long Island in 100 years. We certainly wish them well as we embark on the next 100 years.

A word about our customers: One in particular comes to mind. I volunteer for "Meals on Wheels" occasionally and one of my stops is a woman in her mid-90's living alone. She is still "with it" and very gracious. I once saw a Swezey package in her home and told her who I was. She said she loved Swezey's and had been shopping there since she went with her mother in 1906 (88 years) ago. I told her of our 100th anniversary and she said, "I sure hope you have continued success for another 100 years." The next time I visited her she was reading "How to Get Rich Slowly." She'll probably be wealthy by the time she's 110.

We get lots of letters from our customers. A great majority of them are complimentary. They like our merchandise, enjoy our promotions, but most of all they say, "I love your people." The biggest reason for our continued success is our great staff. This is the thing I am most happy about and most proud of. Because of our people, we have a strong start on the next 100 years.

1994

* The other was Henrietta Acompora, Supervisor of Brookhaven Town.

CHAPTER 36

DAD

I loved my father, and so did just about everyone who knew him. He was tall and slender but broad-shouldered with dark blond hair, a small mustache, hazel eyes and a red nose. A real gentleman, he was kind, generous, warm-hearted and friendly, and usually made you feel good in his presence. "You did a good job." He seldom lost his temper and was quick-witted and quick to act. His one quirk was his abrupt ending of telephone conversations. "Hello, what's going on?" Bang! He had hung up. None of us could beat him to the final click. But it didn't offend anyone. We all knew he was fast and busy and not unkind. And he had a keen sense of humor — sharing slightly off-color stories with friends and associates.

In business, he bought back the department store founded by his father which had been sold out of the family and run down. He worked day and night to make it profitable again.

Dad was a natural merchant, and the business grew and prospered under his leadership. He would say to our buyers, "I want your business so hot it sizzles when I touch it (with best sellers)." And with his encouragement and guidance, the store sizzled.

The resurrection of the family store took its toll. Dad became mentally ill, depressed. Neurasthenic. It was painful to watch and it lasted a dozen years.

I was in high school and then college at the time. I would come home to see him in his chair crying. To see my father sitting and sobbing; I'd feel helpless, despairing and heartbroken. When we went on vacations, he'd cry in the car and cry in the hotels. Our family was desperate. The best psychiatrists were sought. He was admitted to Silver Hill Sanitarium, an upscale retreat for depressants and alcoholics. There was improvement for a while and then it was back to tearful, anguished depression. Shock treatments — he was belted to a bed and electric shocks convulsed his body. He hated it. "Never again." And it terrified the family. "Is it worth it?" — it helped only in the short term.

We knew suicide was in the back of his mind. I would see him go out in the back yard to the swing set and tie the rope around his neck. We would rush out and he'd walk away embarrassed.

During his depressed periods, my mother had to go to the store and help run the business. And he'd go back to the store and be better. For a while.

One night, my wife Nancy and I visited my parents' home. As we left, Dad said, "I can't take it. What will I do?" I murmured something about a visit to Silver Hill. He just shook his head. We hugged him and left. On the way home,

89

silence. Nancy's mother also had bouts of mental illness. We had no ready answers.

The next morning there was an ice storm and I had trouble getting to the store. I got a call from my mother. "Come quickly. I need you." I called a taxi and we slipped and slid to my parents' home. My father had taken an overdose of sleeping pills and was unresponsive. A doctor finally came, but it was too late.

And then we all cried.

What more could we have done?

What a waste of a still young life and such a loving, loved, talented, creative human being.

1999

CHAPTER 37

CHRISTMASTIME IN INDIA (VIA E-MAIL)

Nancy and I have five daughters, two of whom, Karen (Katya) and Trish (Kusumika), live in an ashram in upstate New York. They work there for the Siddha Yoga Foundation, a meditation center which is under the guidance of Gurumayi, a handsome, personable young Indian Guru. Occasionally our daughters go to Ganeshpuri, India, 40 miles north of Mumbai, where the "mother ashram" of Siddha Yoga is located. Karen and Trish went to Ganeshpuri for December and part of January this year and so missed having Christmas with the rest of our family. They e-mailed us their greetings.

12/23/00
Hi Nanna and Poppa!
Thinking of you today as Christmas draws near. I have to tell you, this is an interesting place to celebrate Christmas. We have put up some decorations around. There is an old crooked tree in the dining hall, some fun garlands here and there. The funniest sign of Christmas is down the street at Alex's. Once you step outside the gates, it is dust and beggars and women walking with water on their heads, dogs, you name it. Down the street 100 yards are a few stalls with sort of stores in them. One of them is Alex's. This is where you can get toilet paper, candy, and NOW...Alex's has moved aside a dusty corner for a Christmas section. He sells garlands, cards.... This is how we know it is Christmas in GSP. Alex's has a Christmas section, it's too funny.

Yesterday our children arrived from all over India for our first ever Children's Retreat here. They are so adorable you can't believe it. I love being in the children's area. Today they had their first full day. I think for the most part it was okay, a few first day foibles here and there, but we had an overall good day. Gurumayi came out and chanted with us today. The courtyard was full so I went up to the mandap in the middle of the upper gardens. They had a video feed up there. The wafts of flowers, trees, it smelled like a perfume store...heaven up there...

People travel for hours and hours and hours to get here, even days. They come and often just get a glimpse of Gurumayi, or not sometimes. We are so lucky I can't believe it. But that is all they need, and they take every morsel of it back to their lives.

Anyway, I just wanted to let you know how much I am thinking of you all at this time. Tomorrow night you will be at [Aunt] Prissy's, it will be over. I

91

haven't missed Prissy's in YEARS! I hope Santa comes. Does anyone still believe? My love to all, please, when you meet.

Lots and lots of love to you!!!!! Karen

12/25/00
Dearest Wonderful and Loveable Family,
Merry, Merry, Merry Christmas to you all from Ganeshpuri, India. It is Christmas afternoon here and I hope you get this before Christmas dinner.
It has been a warm, green and peaceful Christmas here. We had a very nice Christmas Eve program last night with three choirs - one was English, second was Hindi, third was children from everywhere. By the time we sang "Silent Night" at the end, the Christmas spirit was high and our minds very peaceful.
This morning Gurumayi spoke at the Christmas program. She has been speaking only Hindi here so we were very happy to have translation for this program...but as things go here the wiring did not work so we listened very carefully to catch a word or meaning here or there. The word we heard again and again was "prem" which means "divine love." Afterwards the Indians were very sweet to share with us what was said. Tonight is caroling in the Amrit and then the men, who are long-term students here, will sing Kawalis, which are Indian devotional songs that are quite dramatic and peppy.
I truly hope you are all doing quite well and enjoying the holiday season. Each day I get more and more excited for those of you who will be travelling to this amazing country soon. Dad, you will be in picture heaven!!! You certainly cannot take any creature comforts for granted after seeing how the people live here. I actually love the simple and pure life here in this ashram.
Big hugs to all of you and wishing you a blessed and joyful New Year.

Love, Trish

12/25/00
Merry Christmas!!! Oh boy, there was sure a moment this morning when I was so missing the loud "ohhs" and "aaahhs" of Christmas morning in the living room. We have had a marvelous day so far. We had a beautiful Christmas program with Gurumayi, lovely singing. She gave a talk on love. Then we had an Indian feast for lunch. Ku and I ate together outside in the gardens. Tonight another western-style feast, then an Indian singing program in the courtyard. Our children from the retreat sang last night in the program. They were so cute. I thought the place was going to stand up and give an ovation. The clapping wouldn't stop for them. Already you can see these little faces lighting up with

the love and excitement of this place. These children are totally wonderful. Some are from prominent, wealthy families, others from Calcutta, etc. are not. I adore all of them. Ku and I were going to send a joint e-mail, but the computers were full when we tried. We both send our love! I never did find a gift for her at Alex's. Poor Ku, she will have to wait. Hope you find something for Daddy!

LOVE LOVE AND LOVE LOVE LOVE!!!!! K

12/30/00

A very belated HAPPY ANNIVERSARY TO YOU and a HAPPY NEW YEAR.

49 years of marriage is certainly an accomplishment these days. I think Dad needs to publish your secret in his book.

Yesterday was a very special day here...It was the first time Gurumayi has given the Siddha Yoga New Year's message talk in India. The Indian devotees came from afar...a twenty hour train ride for the day seems like nothing to them. It was a moment of a lifetime to be there. The message for this year is:

Approach The Present With Your Heart's Consent,
Make It A Blessed Event.

We have a beautiful sign in the courtyard with the message and its image (a shell with a blue pearl inside) with the message written in eight of the Indian languages. I had no idea so many languages are spoken in this country...even the characters are different.

I must admit I am already getting teary eyed about leaving on January 29th. This place and its people has definitely won over my heart.

Love to you!!!!

Trish

12/31/00

Happy, Happy New Year!!! I think today was one of the happiest days of my life. It was the greatest way to end a fabulous year. This morning we took our children on buses to the PRASAD project feeding and art program about twenty minutes from here. There are several charitable programs that the ashram supports and this is one of them. Just the bus ride was like a joy ride. We were on a maybe half-lane road, following bicycles, cows, honking at the dogs to move. The children on the bus were all singing the Christmas carols they learned, half in Hindi, half in English. My smile literally was from ear to ear. Then we arrived at the project. Sundays are children's day. Only children come to eat and then do art. We sat in an open pavilion with about 50-70 local children and our 40 some odd children and chanted as they finished preparing our meal. Then we all lined up and were served a typical Indian meal...no forks or spoons out there...The local children were beautiful. Their shining smiles and their ripped and torn dirty dresses and shirts. They looked at us as though we had landed there from the moon! After we changed and ate, we all went to the pavilion next door. It was a full time art center, where local children come every day to learn art. You should have seen some of the paintings they had displayed. I would have paid $1,000 for one of them! We all did a painting project together then on the bus and home. It reminded me so much of Africa days. I LOVED IT! There is definitely some part of me that is sooo happy in these settings. It was such a rush. I can't get over it. I so wish Mom and Dad could come here and see this all.

We have had one bountiful day after another. Two days ago we took the children to a special Devi Temple near here in Vajreshwari. We had a great guide tell us the fun lore of this town. Then we all hiked up the hill behind the temple. WOWOWOWOW! You have a view of the whole Tansa river valley, including the ashram. There was this wonderful cloud formation circling low surrounding the ashram. It looked like a ring of love around it. Miracles! We all sat at the top of the hill, perched watching the sunset behind the hills. We chanted together, Kali Durqe, as the sun set and then sat quietly together. One of life's great moments.

Yesterday we had stories by one of the old old timers here. He knew Baba before there was any ashram here. We met Dada Yande in a grove by the Durga garden. He sat and told the children these fun stories about Baba. We heard about Baba and the snakes, Baba and the bandits. The kids loved it! When he left they kept yelling BYE DADA BYE DADA!!! It was so dear. He hobbled off with his cane and kept turning back to wave. On my, such memorable moments.

Today there is an all day chant which will take us into the New Year. Of all things, it is raining! I hear it NEVER rains this time of year, and all of us who are here visiting are totally unprepared as we have no umbrellas. We haven't even seen a cloud since we arrived. Every day the weather is perfect. So, I ripped my plastic laundry bag open and am using that in our mid-winter monsoon.

My love to you all!!! Loves and love and blessings from this holy land. Thank you for all you have shared with me in 2000. Wasn't it a great year?! Imagine what 2001 will hold. Happy happy SGMKJ - Karen.

1/01/01

Hi Dad, Happy New Year. It was nice to hear from you!

You are going to be in picture heaven here. I don't think I have ever been anywhere in the world where every person, every sight is a prize photo. Whatever amount of film you were going to bring, double it. I assure you it won't go to waste.

We had the most glorious New Year's message program in the outdoor pavilion in the upper gardens today, then a feast for lunch. Tomorrow is the last day the children are here. We are having a grand finale program with them in the afternoon. It totally made my day having the children run up to me with their hands outstretched to wish me a happy New Year. They are the sweetest! I will miss them. It has been a magical ride going through this retreat with them. They have also totally transformed, they are all a-glow! Such happy faces and shiny hearts, it's really cool. Some of them travelled over 24 hours on train to be here.

Happiest of days, we are surely sending you our love and blessings this and every day.

Wish you were here!   K

1/2/01

Oh, today was the last day. The children spent the morning creating songs, plays, dance to express their experiences of the retreat. This afternoon we invited parents and all the important people we could think of to the finale program. I invited Trish!

The kids were fabulous! It was such a giggle and so heart-warming, too! Then off we went for our final gathering at a tea...ice cream and popcorn galore...then hugs and goodbyes and off they went to all corners of India. They were SHINING when they left! I will miss them terribly.

I went home and showered and now have my sweats on. Going to the big field to watch the sunset. We have the most amazing sunsets here...Tomorrow will rest and clean, then on Thursday I will go to the big city, Mumbai. A pedicure in the Oberoi, swimming at Bridge Candy Pool, a visit to some shops. I am thinking of renting a private car for the day. It would pick me up at the ashram and take me anywhere I want to go all day for $50. It's so funny, that actually sounds like an amazing amount of money. Everything is soooooooo cheap here. The most expensive things are Pringles at Alex's. He gets the equivalent of $2 for Pringles. Somehow you crave stupid American stuff like Pringles once in a while. Good ol' Alex.

Anyhow, bye for now.   K

1/5/01

Trish and I went to Mumbai yesterday. What a scene. We had breakfast in the Oberoi and lunch at the Taj. We felt like we had just landed on the moon. It felt so good just to walk on carpet. It's funny — just a few weeks and we felt so different. India is amazing though. They were building this highway on the way there and all the rocks and dirt were being moved by women, placing the dirt and rocks in baskets on their heads!!! You wouldn't believe it if you didn't see it! I can't believe any highways get built after I saw this. The man in the bulldozer was sleeping. I am sure you will have your fill of stories when you come. On the outskirts of Mumbai, it is slums and slums and slums. People are in front of their plastic bag huts bathing in buckets, dressing, doing it all right on the side of the highway. Cows walk everywhere here, dogs, pigs, goats...naked kids...I have to say. I sure hope you see this side of the country and not just the five star scene. It is a most amazing place. Yesterday in Mumbai, I bought a beautiful ring. It was a flower of peridot. I think I paid $20. I didn't realize how inexpensive fine stones and jewelry are here. If I knew more what I was looking for I may have looked more, but I am probably an easy rip off case. I don't think a thing about stones/jewels. If you covet any diamonds, rubies, etc., this is the place to fulfill your precious jewel fantasies. Anyhow... starting to think about packing. I'll be home before you can say jackrabbit!

See ya' soon! Katya

2001

96

CHAPTER 38

BILL, THE GRAND MARSHALL

St. Patrick's Day Parade, Patchogue, Long Island, March 2000

Bill, our Grand Marshal this year, is adventuresome, compassionate, hard-headed, brave, keen and reverent.

<u>Adventuresome</u> Bill, my nephew, and several other teen-aged boys went with me to the Woodstock Rock Festival. Bill was just recently out of the hospital after having been injured in an auto accident. His mother was not enthusiastic about him going to Woodstock, but he didn't want to miss any of the excitement.

After the first night's concert he slept under the hospital trailer, out of the rain and mud. During the night the trailer collapsed. Bill was not hurt but he did stiffen up and had trouble walking the rest of our stay. This did not stop him from attending each concert and having a wonderful time. Over 30 years later he still talks about his experiences at Woodstock. "After the first day I could hardly move my leg. But it was great! Everyone was sharing their food and pot — though we didn't smoke."

<u>Compassionate</u> Following high school Bill wanted to do something meaningful. He joined the Catholic Relief Service and went to Madagascar, off the coast of Africa. The project was to lay pipes and bring running water to small villages in the outlying bush. He loved his work, made many African friends, and got acquainted with snakes and lemurs. It was a worthy time in his life.

In recent years Bill has done volunteer work for the State University at Stony Brook, Brookhaven Memorial Medical Center, Patchogue Chamber of Commerce and his family foundation which helps over 200 local charitable organizations. All of this in addition to a very active business and social life.

<u>Hard-headed</u> As a youngster Bill used to go on vacation with my family. On one vacation we went swimming in a rocky stream in the mountains of New Hampshire. While playing in the rushing water Bill hit his head on a rock and was knocked unconscious. We looked up and saw him floating downstream in the icy water, out cold. We pulled him out and he soon regained consciousness, but was dizzy. We took him to a local doctor who examined him and said, "He's going to be fine. He's got a hard head."

<u>Brave</u> Bill is President of Swezey's and continually faces the many challenges of a very competitive retail climate. In the past our store opened a new branch every five to ten years. This year, under Bill's leadership, we opened

a new branch, Glen Cove, and are moving and expanding two other stores, Patchogue and Riverhead...three very gutsy moves in a difficult period for an independent family store.

Keen Bill and his lovely wife, Jane, each own a motorcycle and bike around our area in their spare time. It's a keen sight to see them whizzing along the roads in their helmets and leather jackets on their Harleys.

Reverent (well....) I'm the non-working Chairman of the Board at Swezey's and Bill and I get along very well, we have since Woodstock and before. Bill has a good sense of humor. When I recently left the store for a ski trip I asked, "Bill, who's in charge in my absence?" He answered, "Of what?" This may not show reverence, but it does underline his humor and honesty.

2000

CHAPTER 39

EXAMINATION BEFORE TRIAL

I call it tragic — my experience as a bank director of the Union Savings Bank. It was tragic because it involved the untimely deaths of three friends, as well as the demise of the bank. And then I had to testify for two full days as to why I had let it all happen.

My uncle, Hon. Walter Jaycox, had helped found the bank in the 1890's. My grandfather, Walter Rose, was its first, and for a while, only employee. My mother worked at the bank as a young woman and recalled taking in money covered with dirt that local farmers and business people had dug up from hiding places in their backyards.

Union Savings Bank prospered, and, in 1984, as a leading businessman in the area, I was asked to become a trustee. I knew several board members, two of whom served on the local hospital board with me and the president, Paul Fitzpatrick. Paul was a tall, 6'6", outgoing, charming, intelligent man whose previous experience had been as a Merrill Lynch broker and an elected town official.

The early 80's was a time of high prime interest rates — over 10% — and vacillating, so it made it difficult for a savings bank with lots of low-interest mortgages to make money. It had become permissible for savings banks to go into what were called (will I ever forget?) "joint ventures." This meant the bank could partner with contractors or builders to buy land; the bank put up the money and the builder did the construction. Our area was growing and this arrangement became quite common.

Paul and the bank grabbed onto this type of venture with a vengeance. Aside from operating in our local area, we moved into Manhattan, Queens and Staten Island. It became a very profitable business for the bank, and in '87 and '88, we were among the top-earning savings banks in New York State.

In 1989, the real estate market collapsed. In one venture, we thought we had sold almost 300 condos, but a majority of these sales were canceled. Our great plus business of '87 and '88 turned into a big minus business in '89. And within two and one-half years, the Federal Deposit Insurance Company (FDIC) issued a cease and desist order and took over the bank with more than $60,000,000 in real estate ventures gone bad. We were one of 24 banks in our area to go under during the real estate crash.

In the meantime, Paul Fitzpatrick, the architect of our joint ventures, died of a brain tumor in late 1988. He never even got wind of the eventual collapse of his (our) bank. The FDIC, which was bailing out the bank's sour real estate loans from its insurance fund, sold the bank to a more conservative New York savings bank.

Three and one-half years later, the FDIC brought suit against all the trustees, two top real estate loan officers and the legal firm advising the bank, one of whom was also on the bank's board of directors. The suit was for $60,000,000.

We had problems that made this particular case stand out. One of our directors, whom we all trusted, was secretly involved in a real estate deal with a shady joint venture partner. Another director, Chairman of the Real Estate Committee, was doing business on the side with another of our joint venture partners — another conflict of interest. The chief loan officer was caught "flipping" a condo in a joint venture project and making a nice personal profit. We had exceeded our legal lending limits on at least two ventures and the legal firm advising us had allegedly failed to safeguard us adequately.

The suit forced each defendant to get specialized legal counsel to aid in his defense. This turned out to be very expensive.

I had saved all reports that came from the bank so I could refer to them if necessary. I had a stack of papers over five feet high. At one point, when we thought the FDIC was not going to go after the trustees, my wife, Nancy, took it upon herself to dispose of all those papers. She's a neatnick of sorts. A week later, when I was served with the summons, I went to look for some of those bank papers. Talk about a man wanting to cry. If we didn't have an otherwise happy marriage...

After months of legal maneuvering, the defendants and dozens of witnesses were called before the FDIC lawyers — one by one — to testify in an EBT (Examination Before Trial). I was one of the early ones on the list to be questioned. My defense was that I was not on the committee that made the joint venture loans and never voted on any of them. And, of course, I felt the cause of our problem was the swift economic downturn. The recession that hit our area also had a drastic effect on my retail business and a great many other local businesses.

A fellow defendant used the same lawyer. Jack had been a Senior V-P with one of the large accounting firms. He was about the most meticulous and conscientious board member I had served with on any board. And he worked day and night with our lawyer on the defense. Jack also had not been directly responsible for any joint venture.

Two weeks before I was scheduled for the EBT, I had a spinal operation but felt I could testify and wanted to get it over with.

Our lawyer, Nick, was a bright young man who had been at the top of his class at Yale and Yale Law School. Nick had a delightful sense of humor, was a kind young man and appeared to be a lawyer with integrity (an oxymoron?). He prepared me for several hours as best he could for the questioning I would face. His main points were: "Tell the truth and if you can't remember (this had been five to ten years ago), don't hesitate to say so." Also, I had decided that I was not going to point fingers at my co-defendants.

I was not looking forward to this. Two of my fellow trustees had died within two weeks of this time. Lou, who had been President of the Board when the bank collapsed, had developed a serious prostate problem during his tenure at the bank and fought cancer for five years, before he finally succumbed. Dudley, Chairman of our Real Estate Loan Committee, had already testified before the FDIC. When I saw him at Lou's funeral, he said, "It was a bitch!" Two days later, before he finished testifying, he shot himself in the head. Another and most shocking death. There had, of course, been other problems. Dudley had been Lou's best friend and he had gone to see him every day during Lou's last months. Dudley did not have the money for the legal fees — although his fellow directors did help him out. And he had to answer to the government's conflict of interest charge.

Dudley was a good and honest man, father of seven children, a pillar of our local hospital, and a kind and thoughtful person. What a tragedy. After those two deaths, the FDIC decided to continue the suits against their estates.

That was the background when I went in to testify — for two days — up to 16 hours.

The FDIC lawyer, Alan, came into the testimony room and said, "I don't need this; I've got too much else to do." He appeared easygoing and had an infectious smile. He looked like John Cleese, the comedian. He had a rather unkempt moustache around the edges of his lip so that when he sipped coffee, drops of it would remain disconcertingly on his moustache.

The morning questioning seemed to go well. In the afternoon, I began to tire and he began to bear down. He seemed to know about every scrap of paper generated by the bank that came before the board. I did my best to answer his incriminating questions — maybe I tried too hard. Some of my answers were rather convoluted to say the least. "Why were you still making loans to joint ventures when the bank was over the legal lending limit?" I didn't have a quick answer to that, though I did try to give a plausible response, mumbling something about "being between a rock and a hard place." Alan questioned me at length about the problems that had come to light about some of our directors and an officer. I doubt that I shed any new light there but was candid enough to admit I was "surprised, disappointed, shocked and appalled." At the end of the session, neither my lawyer nor I were very happy.

The next morning, my memory was even less sure of itself and I had to give quite a lot of "I don't recalls." Finally, the FDIC lawyer said, surprising Nick and me, "That's all the questions I have." Nick requested a two-hour break, after which he wanted to question me to hear my side.

We returned that afternoon and, although Nick's questions were supposed to be softballs, I had trouble with some of them. However, a defense of the actions of the board did come out. At Nick's prodding, I got in that I was over 70 and "my memory wasn't as sharp as it had been five or ten years ago." After an hour, Nick was finished with me.

The FDIC lawyer, at this point, seemed very agitated. He said in a severe voice, unlike his previous demeanor, "Mr. Swezey, I now have 90 minutes more of questions for you."

We adjourned for a few minutes and neither Nick nor I could figure out what had upset Alan. His questioning became intense and belligerent. He seemed to lose his cool. At one point, he raised his voice and said, "As a director, weren't you responsible for <u>all</u> that went on at the bank?" My denial of this "all" and my "I'm sorry, I can't recalls" eventually quieted him down and, in 45 minutes, he put a stop to the inquisition.

On the way out, Alan put his hand on my shoulder and said, "You weren't bad, Mr. Swezey. It was your lawyer that got me going."

That part was over for me, but the case would drag on for many more very expensive months; 95% of these cases are eventually settled before trial.

But we had already lost the bank and, much worse, three fine men died.

1998

CHAPTER 40

INNOCENT!

They had been after us for four years. And we, most of us, were innocent! Innocent!

We were on the board of a bank, a bank started by my uncle, and my grandfather was the first employee. For 75 years it was a successful, respected bank, and only ten years ago, one of the most profitable savings banks in New York State. We were heavily into real estate joint ventures — JV's. Lots of profit, lots of money. Then, bang — the real estate economy tanks and goes to hell. Twenty-two banks fail in our area. We fail, go under. It was the pits - devastating, embarrassing and deflating. As James Carville said, "It was the economy, stupid — the economy."

But did the FDIC (Federal Deposit Insurance Corp.) see it that way? Hell, no! They fought us for four years, with enormous legal fees, 125 depositions, no concern for culpability, what's right, what's fair. We failed. "The taxpayers anteed up and you pay!"

And what happened to us? Lou died slowly and agonizingly of prostate cancer; Fitz succumbed to a brain tumor; Dudley committed suicide. The FDIC went after everyone — the families of the deceased and us, the survivors.

We fought! "It's not fair. It's not right. They can't do this to innocent people." The legal bills mounted. The FDIC kept coming, relentlessly, with all the power of the federal government and its unlimited money.

And what did our lawyers say? New York City lawyers at $350 an hour. "Settle. Settle or else. It's going to a jury trial. You know what that means. Your case is strong but could go either way. Twelve postmen doing their fucking duty, protecting the taxpayers. Hey, a trial can cost two hundred thousand and eight weeks of your life. Settle!"

What did it do to us? We fought among ourselves. Ed wouldn't talk to Jack. Jack raged at Steve. Steve slammed down on Jack, everyone pointed fingers at Charlie. God! It's made us all animals, and who was winning? The government and the lawyers.

So we hung our heads and, for a big pot of money, we settled. We were in the right but they won. The BASTARDS.

1999

103

CHAPTER 41

JULIETTE AND MARK

Pierce has a crush on Juliette. Pierce is a seventy-plus retired dentist, my former college roommate, and every time I see him he talks about the lovely and talented Juliette. Who is she? She's the Oscar-winning French actress Juliette Binoche, a star in "The English Patient" and numerous other movies. Juliette was coming to Broadway to appear in a Pinter play, "Betrayal." As soon as Pierce heard the news, he called and ordered four tickets — in the second row. Nancy and I were happy to go with Pierce and his wife Lois. I, too, find Juliette very appealing.

When the curtain goes up, Juliette is sitting at a table, less than ten feet from us, sipping wine with a former lover. Both are married to others and discuss dejectedly why their affair is not working. Ms. Binoche is wearing no make-up and is obviously unhappy. In this scene she is a handsome woman but not the least glamorous. We are at eye level with her shoes, which show absolutely no wear on the soles. (Pinter plays are noted for little action.) The following eight scenes go backward in time and in each one Juliette wears a touch more make-up and appears happier. In the final scene, when she first meets her lover, she is absolutely luscious in a low cut bright red dress and matching liptstick. She has an anticipatory glow. This is the Juliette we had come to see and she surely didn't disappoint. I asked Pierce two questions — "Were you close enough?" (I had teased him about not getting first row seats.) He smiled broadly. "Did she meet your expectations?" "You know it!"

"Betrayal" has a cast of only four. We were surprised and pleased to find that we knew one of the actors, Mark Lotito, who is from our hometown, Sayville.

Our friend Mark has a small part in the play, an Italian waiter in a scene with Juliette's husband and lover. We all agreed he was just fine. We had seen him on Broadway in a bigger part in a revival of "Most Happy Fella."

Twenty years ago I had interviewed Mark for Dartmouth College. He was a scholar and football player in our high school and was readily admitted to Dartmouth. We saw him several times at the college and his interest in football waned as his new-found interest in acting blossomed. When he graduated, he applied and was accepted to law school. The acting bug had him and he left for New York City to test his talents. Mark's parents were devastated. His father, who had been in my high school class, went on to become a school principal. He and his wife, Loretta, were looking forward to having a lawyer in the family. Not

Mark. He waited on tables, got bit parts here and there and eventually made a living on the stage and in television.

After the play, we debated about going backstage to see Mark and perhaps even meet you know who. In the lobby, we bumped into Mark leaving the theatre. After a warm greeting, our first question was, "What about Ms. Binoche?" Mark — "I'm not in any scene with her but she seems like a lovely person and a fine actress. She's excited about her latest movie, 'Chocolat.'" Pierce — "Didn't I see you on TV recently?" "Yes, I've been in several episodes of 'Law and Order' and other cop shows." "How's your wife?" (He is married to the actress Valerie Wright.) "We have a five-week-old baby and Valerie is on maternity leave from 'Annie Get Your Gun.' "Are your parents reconciled to your life in the theatre?" "Not yet, but they love their new grandson." Mark was charming and friendly and we chatted for another ten minutes. Finally it was time to say "Our best to your new family and please say hello to Juliette from some ardent admirers."

A month later Nancy and I watched "Damage," a Juliette movie that Pierce had enthusiastically recommended. My God! Throughout the movie Nancy kept saying, "Oh Pierce. Oh Pierce." Juliette and her co-star Jeremy Irons had four scenes of sexual daliance. Adultery. Each one steamier than the preceding one. In the final sexual scene they are both nude, going at it with great ardor and athleticism. "Oh Pierce." "Oh Juliette!"

2000

CHAPTER 42

DARTMOUTH

FOR OUR FIFTIETH REUNION

Dartmouth has had a strong and positive influence on my life. I met my wife Nancy at Dartmouth. She roomed with my sister Priscilla ('49 Carnival Queen) at nearby Colby-Sawyer. Nancy and I are Protestants and lived next door to a Catholic Church, and have six children and now six grandchildren.

Our first child is John and then ten girls in a row — five wonderful daughters and five exciting granddaughters. And finally a grandson, Thomas. He was born autistic. Thanks to the newest methods of therapy, Thomas, at two and a half, can look me straight in the eye and say, "Hello, Poppa." I think God made grandchildren to bring special joy to people over 50. The only thing better than a big family is a bigger family. At our last gathering there were 39 of us.

My whole business career was as a buyer and then president of our 105-year-old family department store. We now have five locations. I have retired and turned the reins over the fourth generation, my son John, a fine retailer, and two nephews. The climate for the family retailer gets tougher all the time as the big guys get bigger and more powerful, but we're still hanging in there.

As a retiree, I enjoy working with our local church — a liberal-minded Congregational Church that has been in the forefront of civil, women's, gay and lesbian rights. Being on a hospital board in today's changing medical world is an interesting challenge. My passions: Family, photography, ballet, twentieth century art, and now, thanks to 1950's Joe Medicott, memoir writing — especially about "The Joys and Jolts of Retirement."

We visit Hanover several times a year — football weekends and a week in the summer. Recently, I've been meeting my college roommate, Dick Udall, for the week-long Alumni College. I am most impressed with both the faculty and the undergraduates at Dartmouth. Nancy and I have enjoyed several Dartmouth-sponsored trips — China and Africa. Everything was first rate.

Hopes for the future: Continued good health and happiness for family and friends, a perpetually strong stock market, a resurgence of Dartmouth football and a cure for, among other things, baldness.

2000

CHAPTER 43

DARTMOUTH SNAPSHOTS

Fifty Years Ago

I remember playing touch football with Eddie Leeds before he became The Ed Leeds (Dartmouth's premier basketball player). His football suggestion was "Short high passes — basketball style."

———

My thesis professor was Professor McCallum — tall, long, thin face, auburn haired — gentle but firm. In spite of numerous corrections he gave me a good mark on the thesis "David Dubinsky and ILGW." Professor McCallum's son, Bill, was in my class.

———

I used to go to dances in the basement of the white church. One of my favorite partners was Professor Bagley's attractive daughter. I had Professor Bagley for my French course, a warm, friendly man with no French accent. When I was confined to Dick's House (infirmary) for a spell, he was the only professor to visit me. I had wished it had been his daughter.

———

Professor Bruce taught government and he was a terror. Rumor had it that he had lost a son in the war and was taking it out on those of us who returned. During every class, he would question several class members on the day's assignment. God help those who couldn't answer accurately. Much of your mark depended upon it.

———

I ruptured my spleen playing tackle football and ended up in Dick's House — a wonderful place for rehabilitation. They had lovely, friendly nurses whom I saw daily for two weeks. One in particular, Ellen, a pert, petite blonde, took great care of all of us. She worried constantly about her husband who was fighting in the Battle of the Bulge in Germany.

I recall our favorite pastime at Dick's house was looking out the windows toward the student nurses' dorm next door — hoping to catch a glimpse as they dressed or undressed. Sometimes they would "forget" to pull down the shades and we would luck out.

————

In the Great Issues Course some great speakers that stood out for me were Dean Atcheson — smooth and articulate about foreign policy; Reinhold Niebuhr — fascinating theologian; Robert Frost — such a witty, creative, original mind; and Richard Nixon — a bubbly young Representative who spoke passionately of the Alger Hiss case.

————

A roommate, who has asked to remain anonymous, was on the cross-country team. He needed money so one day he sold some of his blood to the local blood bank and then ran cross-country. They carried him back to the room. (Dr. U.)

————

Professor Egerer was a short, chubby man and a lively lecturer in the English Department. He was gay before it was more socially acceptable. When I went to graduate school at N.Y.U., I saw that he was then teaching there.

————

Herb West — Comp Lit Professor — was an interesting man and a notorious soft touch. If you asked for a conference, told him you liked Henry Miller (i.e. "I love Henry Miller"), and asked for an A, you'd get it. I did and he did.

————

Music Professor Lawlor was a terrible pianist. When he played the class would laugh and then become unruly. He got mad and gave us an extra assignment — "Write a two-page essay on Mozart." They were graded: six pages or more got an A, 4-5 pages a B, and 2-3 pages a C.

————

Old Professor Murch (Physics) was a humorless, dry lecturer, but got your attention by locking the classroom door at the dot of 8:00 am, so no one could come in late.

————

Classmate Al Tarr, whom I often sat next to because of our last names, was a handsome, bright, soft-spoken young man and poet. He was killed in the Korean War.

————

I had two dates for Senior Green Key. I was with Connie for Thursday and Friday (bright as a brass button with beautiful brown eyes and luscious lips). Then she was passed along to my friend Don, and I had Pam my hometown gal for Saturday and Sunday. I really liked Connie, but she got along too well with Don — such were the vagaries of young love.

————

Lectures and seminars with Robert Frost were memorable. He had a shock of white hair and a New England drawl. He gave monologues about everything from the Boston Red Sox to his days at Dartmouth. And then would "say" his poems. He had the most original mind of anyone I've met, funny and a joy to be around.

————

Al Foley — I never had him but often heard his humorous Vermont stories. A classmate took pot shots at his house with a BB gun from across the Connecticut River. (R.D.)

————

Professor Demaree — History — was a sweet-tempered professor who made history come alive by making the important figures of the day come alive. In '48, we speculated on the Republican nominee for President. I favored Senator Vandenburg (sign on his desk, "This too shall pass"). Professor Demaree correctly predicted Thomas Dewey (and also thought he would be elected. Harry gave him hell).

————

French Professor Denoeu had a twinkle in his eyes and quite an accent and is remembered for singing French operatic arias in class "Ah Fuyey Douce Image." I have been an opera buff ever since.

———————

When I return to Dartmouth and classes are in session, I wonder how in hell we ever managed without women on campus. Or why.

1997

CHAPTER 44

FIFTY RETURNS

One-third had died, one-third chose not to attend, and one-third of the Dartmouth Class of 1950 returned to Hanover for the 50th reunion. My closest classmate and friend, Peirce Udall, was struck by a car while bicycling and was recuperating in a hospital, but for the 200 plus who went, it was a reunion of warm friendships renewed, fine camaraderie and exciting memories.

Before the reunion each class member was asked to write 600 words or so about his life after graduation. This was put in book form and produced a symphony of joys and jolts, laughter and tears over the last 50 years:

"I was a banker but they wouldn't allow me to lend any money because I was too good-natured."

"I have found it and it's the most precious gift we could ever have – it's love: Love of Dartmouth, love of Country, love of music, singing, poetry, family, friends and an 18-year-old Prison Ministry."

"Tailgate parties, coal-fired stoves and frozen diapers on the laundry line left sweet memories of life before mortgages, tuition and sensitivity training."

"I have had Alzheimer's for a number of years and live in a nursing home, but I don't know it." (Written by a brother)

"Married since '61 to a gorgeous, artistically talented and angelic New Yorker."

"The Biblical Word of God is our mainstay and blessing in life, and we trust in God's great saving grace (unmerited favor) through our Lord and Savior Jesus Christ."

"I have learned one thing: no more weddings, no more divorces. Men are from Mars and women are from the Yellow Pages."

"I lost my beloved wife of 43 years to cancer, and my only sister-in-law also to cancer. My brother passed away suddenly. Then I met an absolutely outstanding woman. We lived together for 3 1/2 years until a cerebral hemorrhage took her from me."

"I commuted on a bike during my last years at the C.I.A."

"You can find me neck-deep in sawdust and bark."

"My Dartmouth education brought a richness to my life beyond measure."

"I had the opportunity to free Rubin 'Hurricane' Carter after 20 years in prison."

"After 38 years as an equity analyst and bond guru, I still can't figure out where the market is headed."

"Thanks to nepotism I became president in 1959."

"I have known love, fierce loyalty and fascinating work, as well as betrayal, hate and failures."

"My first wife exulted over the phone, 'I never loved you. I never even liked you.'"

"I am grateful to be able to write these words."

And then, of course, the glories of children and grandchildren. As Garrison Keillor says, "All above average."

The first night of the reunion was a head-spinner. It was difficult to get to sleep after all those intimate and entertaining conversations with men I hadn't seen in fifty years. "Spent the night in jail," "My present wife," "China was a blast," "Negotiated with the Soviet Union," "My wife is a minister," "My main recreation was sex," "I Woke Up Screening," "I graduated under a cloud," "Ugly divorce," "Prostate cancer support group."

The second evening the Dartmouth Glee Club performed at a more accomplished level than I had remembered in 1950. This time the group had the advantage of having women. Their soprano voices added a special sparkle and beauty. When I asked several classmates, former Glee Club members, if the women were an asset to the music, they hedged, "I liked the sound of the all-male voices."

I also asked several returnees if they would consider going to a single-sex college again. "Well I sure did enjoy Dartmouth." My personal reaction today is, "Never in a million years." However I did marry a student from nearby Colby-Sawyer, a major plus, and Dartmouth has served me well for over fifty years.

At the Class luncheon Joe Medlicott, who has done so much for our class – editing our class newsletter for over thirty years and putting together the 420-page reunion yearbook – gave the fifty year address. He touched on some contentious topics with tact and understanding. Why were some of our children accepted at Dartmouth and others not? Bud's six children went to Dartmouth. None of my six did, although two applied. He also spoke of the declining quality of fraternity life and why the administration is thinking of phasing out fraternities.

Jim Wright, President of the College, then spoke but appeared a little gun-shy on the sensitive topics. His most memorable words on referring to our class were from Mae West, "It's not the men in your life but the life in your men."

A class seminar was led by six of our most successful graduates. Judge Lee Sarokin spoke of the eroding public confidence in our judicial system. "But it's still the best in the world." Investment whiz Rick Miller noted that most of our top companies are less than thirty years old, while in Europe the top companies are all over thirty. Noted playwrite, Frank Gilroy, remarked that good work in theater today is done Off Broadway and away from New York. Dr. Jim Strickler spoke of the Genome Project and its implications in choosing a partner, privacy, employment and better drugs for cancer and hypertension. World renowned ecologist George Woodwell's topic covered the problems of population – two billion people in 1950 and ten billion by 2010.

There was a reception at Baker Library for Honorary Degree Recipients and our class was asked to attend. Two of our 50's classmates, Don Hall and Norm McCulloch, were receiving honorary degrees, along with Hank Aaron, Mrs. Ted Geisel (Dr. Seuss) and Dr. Shirley Ann Jackson, President of R.P.I. There was a long line for the reception so I cut in with a classmate I knew. Mistake number one. We got in quickly but Hank Aaron hadn't arrived yet. At the end of the receiving line, a bit away from the others, was a young, attractive blonde woman. I thought, "Just another pretty face from the library," so I ignored her. Mistake number two. I later found out she was J.K. Rowling of Harry Potter fame, the hottest young author in the history of publishing. I have been kicking myself ever since. Later I learned a classmate, also a writer, asked her the key to writing for children. "Think like a child," she answered. Not greeting Ms. Rowling bothered me so I went back to the library to shake her hand. As I arrived, classmates were leaving in disgust. They had waited 45 minutes to meet the Honorees, only to be told the reception was over. Not good.

At our final class banquet the scheduled speaker was Art Buchwald, the humorist/columnist. He is about our ages (b. 1925), so he could be considered an honorary classmate. At the last minute, he decided to join the classmates "who chose not to attend." No explanation was given. Not very humorous, not very honorary.

As I returned to the Inn to pack and leave, I saw a classmate, Bob, with a two-year-old in a stroller. I asked if the young lady was his grandchild. "No," he replied. "First generation." Three cheers for the Class of 1950.

ADDENDUM

There were two hundred women at the reunion and, when I went through the Honorees' Reception line, I spoke to Don Hall of Hallmark fame about his wife, Adele. In Don's autobiography, he said she is Kansas City's leading volunteer worker and has a national reputation for her service to causes, especially pertaining to children. I kiddingly suggested to Don that perhaps Adele should be the one up for an honorary degree. He agreed and asked if I wanted to meet her. She was seated nearby so I went over for a chat.

Adele Hall is a charming lady, who was wearing a sleek, neat, yellow dress. I asked her what she thought of Hillary Clinton's work with children. Adele smiled and said she felt Hillary was sincere and helpful.

When I mentioned that I thought Bill Clinton, in spite of his problems, had done a good job as President and now seemed to be very popular, Adele demurred, "Well, you know, we're really good friends of the Bushes."

2000

CHAPTER 45

FIFTY YEARS LATER

My wife Nancy and my sister Priscilla roomed together at Colby-Sawyer College. The classic story. I married my sister's roommate. I also dated other girls at Colby-Sawyer and had many exciting memories of the young ladies there — so close to Dartmouth when they were both single-sex colleges.

Nancy, Pris and I went back to Colby-Sawyer for their 50th reunion. Not having seen most of those people since graduation, I was shocked. They weren't the young, perky, flirtatious, smiling, self-conscious students that I remembered so vividly. My wife and sister had aged slowly and gracefully. These women went from 20 to 70 in one gigantic leap. It was a disappointing jolt. And where were some of my old favorites — button-nosed, sexy Tracy, the Paris bombshell Gisele, friendly, passionate Jean and flaming redheaded skiing friend Ann? Different class, distance, indifference and death had kept some of my favorites away.

Those who did come were most cordial, enthusiastic, white-haired and gently wrinkled.

We went to a reception at the President's house. I was startled by a young (thirtyish) dark-haired, tall and most attractive woman who appeared in the garden. It turned out to be the president, Ann Ponder. She was a clear-headed and forceful speaker, and we seemed to take to her as soon as we met her. The key to her message was alumnae have made a difference and the future of the college is, with everyone's help, bright. The next day there were several meetings and a class banquet. Nancy, Pris and I decided everyone looked better the second day. I would guess that they felt the same about us. The chat topics were trips, grandchildren, volunteering, golf and, my favorite topic, "Sex Over Sixty." When a friend was asked what she did for excitement, she said, "Absolutely nothing." Another: "Raised four kids, got my divorce and now living the good life." We were relieved that no one dwelt on matters of health. Promises of "getting together soon" and "staying in good health" ended two days of remembrances, embraces and the joy of being together again. "Colby Forever."

1999

CHAPTER 46

ASYA

My typist was a Muslim. And we became friends.

At a summer writing course I took at Dartmouth, computer illiterates were given a list of students who wanted to make extra money typing. I scanned the list for names of people I thought would be exciting to meet. How about Asya Mu Min? I thought maybe Indonesian or Thai. No — she came from the Brownsville section of Brooklyn — and was partly African-American, Native American and German. She practiced the Islamic religion and wore the headdress of that faith. A tallish, slim, good-looking young woman, she wore a green Dartmouth tee shirt with the numerals "00" and had a big, relaxed smile.

Asya was close to her mother, a seamstress, and unaware of her father's whereabouts. She had eight siblings, one of whom was a student at the University of Pennsylvania.

She had attended the local Brownsville high school, got all A's and was considered "the smartest student they ever had." Accepted at Stanford, Yale, Harvard, M.I.T. and Dartmouth, she chose Dartmouth because of its rural setting.

Asya's life at Dartmouth has not been a happy experience. She's fond of the professors and the location but she's encountered problems with some fellow students and the administration. "They don't listen." Her boyfriend Paul is Caucasian and some of her African-American friends have abandoned her because of this. And her Brooklyn high school did not prepare her well for a challenging education, especially in the sciences. Unlike many other students she had no Advanced Placement courses. I asked if she'd encountered racism at Dartmouth. "Oh no." Asya is bright and dedicated and determined and her goal is to be a neurosurgeon. She has wanted to be a doctor since she was five.

One of the other participants in my summer course was a surgeon, so I arranged that he and Asya and I have lunch together. She told us briefly of her faith. She likes the discipline of Islam, is a vegetarian and keeps her body covered.

The surgeon, Dr. Carter, on the staff of Albany Medical School, gave her some practical advice for applying to med school. "Don't say you want to be a surgeon. Most interviewers are internists or family practitioners and might not appreciate that. And have a good answer for the question. 'What will you do if you don't get into medical school?'" She didn't have a ready answer but would think about it.

Asya was a good typist, quick, accurate and helpful. We usually met around 10:30 at night in the lobby of the Hanover Inn where I was staying. We sat together and went over what I had just written. She seemed to enjoy my writing, but not my penmanship. I was writing on topics she was not familiar with but found interesting — a trip to Las Vegas with my daughter, meeting Warren Buffett and sex over sixty. She would laugh and say, "Oh wow."

One evening she brought Paul. He was a student at Dartmouth, was taking a year off to work and visited her every weekend. Paul was tall, blond and handsome with an all-American look. Las Vegas interested him so we chatted about "O" one of the casino shows I had written about. "It sounds real neat." When Asya and Paul left, arm-in-arm, they made a striking, head-turning couple.

As I paid her and we parted for the last time, I asked if she'd like to meet my wife when we would be back for a football game. She gave me a big, relaxed smile and said, "I'd love to." Then to my surprise and joy she said, "Kim, may I give you a hug?"

1999

CHAPTER 47

THE GOLDEN GIRL

Our teacher is a big guy — an oversized teddy bear but with a dark side. He has a ponytail and wears shorts, tee shirts and sandals to class. Terry is a professor of English at Dartmouth College and was giving a course on memoir writing for Alumni College. He is personable, outgoing and a fascinating lecturer. After our morning class we met with him one-on-one. He'd put his bare feet on his desk and give us helpful and thoughtful critiques on our work. His language was salty, to say the least and at one point, he made a suggestion for an essay I was writing. When I showed him how I had used his suggestion, he said, "that was f———g brilliant."

Terry read us part of a memoir he was working on. It was about his struggle with depression and how his walks in the woods helped him fight it. This was a glimpse of his dark side, the only one we saw or heard. His humor, clear-headed thinking and warm-hearted helpfulness impressed each of us and by the end of the course we all loved him.

Terry's class had people from their 30's to their 80's: a school teacher; a handsome older woman; a close relative of Greta Garbo; a businessman-father of six teenagers; and a management consultant who said he had "not a single happy memory of growing up." And finally, there was Diana.

She is Diana Golden Brosnihan, a celebrated ski champion, and she wrote and spoke with great passion and brilliance about the tremendous peaks and valleys of her young life. She is a pale, thin-faced woman with piercing brown eyes, who speaks with clear diction as if she'd had speech training. She was wearing earrings in the shape of the Chevrolet symbol — the explanation was that her husband had an old Chevy coupe that he cherished. Diana has only one leg and was on crutches.

During the class discussions, Diana was friendly and encouraging as we each read something we had written. She said to me, "I love your humor and descriptions." She was the last to read her work to our class, and it was a bombshell.

Hers was the most compelling, heart-rending story I'd ever heard. When she was twelve, she lost a leg to bone cancer. Soon after, she began to ski and eventually became an Olympic Gold Medalist, winning 19 golds in world and national competitions. She was the first disabled athlete given the "Athlete of the Year" award by the U.S. Olympic Committee and was recently elected to the Skiing Hall of Fame. Diana was Golden.

After ski racing, Diana became an inspirational speaker and started her own business, "Golden Opportunities." She toured the country on her crutches wearing her Olympic Gold Medal and giving pep talks.

Then the cancer returned. First Diana lost a breast, then the other, followed by her uterus. The loss of the fourth part of her body overwhelmed her. "It was not the holocaust of my body that was the worst. It was the fall from grace that accompanied it. The crumbling of my mind."

Diana took an overdose of pills but then realized she wanted to live and, deeply depressed, ended up in a psychiatric hospital. Two hospitalizations, group therapy, a visit to Esalan in California and the companionship of a friendly pet Alaskan Malamute all helped turn her life around. Then one day Diana ran into a former Dartmouth classmate. Steve is a cartoonist who works with hospitalized children. They dated and eventually married, bringing a degree of joy and happiness back into her life. However, Diana now has cancer in a dozen spots in her body and is on periodic chemotherapy. "Treatable but not curable." As Diana reached the end of her story, she broke down. And there was not a dry eye in the class. Terry approached her and put his arm around her and said, "Let's just sit quietly for a few minutes."

I was stunned by this story of devastation and courage — of reaching the heights and depths and still pulling herself up to have a positive, hopeful, encouraging attitude.

Later Diana told us that she admired the example of the older people in our class who, like her, were reaching the twilight of their lives but were optimistic and seemed to be making the most of their remaining time.

Toward the end of our class week, we read our second papers. Diana wrote "Weird Play," filled with black humor. She broke up in laughter as she read it. She told us that it was "the black humor that keeps me sane." She told of going to a party and suggesting they play "Pin the body parts on Diana." Even her loving husband thought that a bit warped. The reaction of our class to this second essay was muted. It was unexpected and we smiled but we were still blown away by her first presentation.

Diana then told our class the reactions of children to her one leg. She said that three-year-old kids begin to notice and become intrigued and questioning.

"Did you lose it somewhere?"
"What do you do with the other shoe?"
"What did they cut it off with?"
"Was there much blood?"

Diana got a kick out of telling us this and laughed again.

The class went out to dinner together and Diana and I were partners at the table. We talked about her recent trip to Barcelona, a city of beauty and joyfulness. Then we spoke of Italy. I had given a piece in class on a photographic course I had taken in a small town in Tuscany. The final day was devoted to photographing a nude, and I had bought a bouquet of flowers for the model, which she held in front of her naked body as I snapped away. Diana commented favorably on this. So at our dinner together she took a bouquet of flowers out of the vase on the table and held it in front of her chest. "Kim — take my picture."

Diana left the dinner early; she had chemotherapy that day and was feeling shaky. Before she left she told us that Steve and she were planning to take ballroom dancing lessons when they got home. They wanted to learn to do "The Hustle."

The Golden Girl with the will of iron left town shortly after. I prayed that her future would continue to give her many more moments of hope and joy.

1998

CHAPTER 48

MEALS ON WHEELS

Meals on Wheels is a charity that helps feed middle-class shut-ins. I've volunteered once a week for five years. We pick up hot and cold meals at the local hospital and deliver them to people who are aged, infirmed or shut-ins. I certainly can't say we feed the poor. It is a no-brainer, but I've learned a lot. And it's been quite an attitude adjustment. Shut-ins are not shut-outs. They're very much alive.

As in most endeavors the most fascinating aspects are the people one meets. I've had some interesting "clients." One lovely old lady in her 90's was reading a book, "How to Get Rich Slowly."

A man in his 70's, a former scientist, lived alone in a pleasant but extremely cluttered house. Books, papers, mail and vitamin pills filled the place. On top of one pile was a book entitled "Avoiding Clutter." And we soon learned he still likes the women. He made a pass at my partner.

Another man, a former school custodian, was always standing and pacing when we arrived. He wasn't hungry but liked to talk — especially about his World War II experiences. He'd been on four Italian and North African invasions and loved each one. "Some of the men were peeing their pants, but I really liked them invasions. I even volunteered for them."

For a short time my partner was a N.Y.C. fireman out on disability. One of my clients, a relative of mine, said to him, "I bet you love those parades." He just smiled.

And then there is Gisele. She is my delivery partner. When I first met her she had a slight accent. I thought, hopefully, she was French. Then she told me she was born in Germany. Her stepfather came to America for a job — not to escape oppression.

I am a waspy-wasp and don't believe I have many prejudices. I like gays and lesbians (our minister is a lesbian), Jews (brother-in-law), the French (except French waiters), Native Americans (admiration and sorrow), ballet dancers (love 'em), African-Americans (Michael, not O.J.) and Canadians (the nicest). However, I have strong feelings about Germans and not good ones.

I've read a number of books and articles about the Holocaust (by Carlo Levi and Elie Weisel), Thomas Keneally's "Schindler's List" and Daniel Goldhagen's "Hitler's Willing Executioners." Each one is more maddening than the last. How could this have happened in a supposedly Christian nation? I'm still a Christian but this Holocaust reading has changed how I believe in God. No Benevolent Presence there.

A short visit to Germany did nothing to dispel my concerns about Germans. I was hosted by a retail executive in Frankfurt and at one point he began talking about the Turks, who do much of the common labor today in Germany. "They smell bad. They eat peculiar food and they're quite a problem for Germany." "Quite a problem." I remembered the solution to another "quite a problem" they had.

When this host left the room, his assistant, a woman, said, "German men are single-minded. They have tunnel vision. It could happen again." This was the only reference to the Holocaust I heard while I was in Germany.

So I was disappointed when I heard that Gisele is from Germany. I have lots of friends whose ethnic background is German. This hasn't bothered me, but native Germans have been a Christian challenge for me.

Gisele is a friendly, attractive, very pleasant brunette who seems to be popular with all the other Meals on Wheels volunteers. She is obsessive about cleanliness (aren't all Germans?) and she notices every speck of dirt on my quite new Mercury that we use for delivery. "Kim, is that a new scratch?" she'd say in a kidding way as she gently rubbed her fingers over the spot. Her car, which we don't use, is absolutely spotless.

Occasionally Gisele speaks about her life in Germany as a young girl. She recalled running into a wine cellar as French planes came over to strafe her town. She hardly knew her real father — only remembered him as a soldier walking down the street in his German army uniform. He died of starvation in a Russian concentration camp when she was about nine.

Gisele and I get along very well. We tease each other and laugh a lot. Sometimes we bet on the age of a client. "Another buck, Kim, I'm tired of losing." She is a most caring person. We are not supposed to get involved with our clients but she checks them closely each week, chats with them and does whatever little can be done to make their lives more pleasant.

And when I have a problem she is most thoughtful. Occasionally I'd have a bad back and she insisted on carrying all the trays herself. I learned that she also volunteered in nursing homes.

None of this surprises me. There are kind, thoughtful, caring people from all parts of the world. Millions of them, even in Germany, but Gisele helped me diminish my anti-German sentiments. I told her this. She smiled broadly and said nothing. The next week she brought me a bag of a special licorice she knew I enjoyed.

I still read about the Holocaust. I'm still devastated by it, but thanks to Gisele I'm trying hard not to hold it against the German people. Meals on Wheels has helped give me food for thought on being more tolerant.

1998

CHAPTER 49

S.O.S. (SEX OVER SIXTY)

Several years ago, one of the buyers in our store — she was in her late 70's — said, "Sex at my age is like trying to get a marshmallow into a piggy bank." I laughed, <u>hard</u>, but then thought: Is that what I'm facing in a few years?

I asked a number of my friends if they would comment on "sex over sixty." Some of the responses were funny, some sad and some straight on.

"It needs to be put on the calendar."
"Great whenever."
"Is there such a thing?"
"When I wake up I think of sex. My wife thinks of coffee."
"It's marvelous," she said sarcastically as she limped away crippled with arthritis, a bad back and a confessed need for Viagra.
"My wife has lost interest but I <u>THINK</u> about it a lot."
"It's like feeding spaghetti to a lion."
"We favor matinees, we're too tired at night."
"My husband likes sex and carrots — he doesn't know which comes first."
"Once a year — without fail."
"I'm 72 and on my second marriage and never knew sex could be such fun."
And then there was that marshmallow.

My mother, who lived to be a healthy 93, was fond of saying, "Use it or lose it." I doubt very much if she was referring to the reproductive organs — or maybe she was — but I have made a strong effort to follow her advice.

We do hear and read about suggestions for a better sex life all the time. Bob Dole has found the cure for "erectile dysfunction." And the look on his face in the ad for Viagra is smug surprise. "Was that me?" He still can't believe it. His wife Liddy's expression is "I'm sexy enough to be President." But her hairdo needs attention.

Mark McGwire, the home-run king, takes ASD (androstenedione). The body — so the ad goes — immediately converts it to testosterone — "the prime producer of your sexual abilities." We'd all like to hit more home runs. (But do we want those biceps?)

And now I read that a nutrient in tomatoes is very important for sexual health. It's called "lycopene" (pronounce that without a chuckle). Aside from its sexual helpfulness, Dr. Clinton (that's his name) of the Harvard Medical School says lycopene (he pronounces it lie-co-pea-knee) is a strong player in deterring heart disease and prostate tumors. What more could you ask? Ketchup on everything.

All sexologists recommend plenty of exercise — all your muscles and constantly. "They" say the activity of intercourse is helpful for arthritis. That beats gold shots, copper bracelets and Advil.

Would you believe that in my research I turned up something called the "Position of the Decade." This was in an article in "Men's Health" on "Sex — The 50's and Beyond." "Your erections will be stronger in an UPRIGHT position — standing, kneeling or sitting." Standing — now there's a position to ponder. Tiptoes? Knees bent? I'm not sure that's the position of the decade when in your 70's. George Bernard Shaw said about sex: "The pleasure is momentary. The position is ridiculous." Was he talking about upright?

Of course, everyone agrees (I hope) that the most important part of the body for a good sex life is your brain. To quote that noted philosopher, Yogi Berra, "Ninety percent of this game is half mental." That's as good an equation as any for the connection between mind and body that it takes to play any game.

A recent movie I saw at an alumni college course was a Brazilian flick called, "O Amor Natural." It's a lighthearted documentary about desire and age. Older people read aloud erotic verses by a Brazilian poet. In their 60's to 80's, these people are delighted by what they read and confide their own tales of flings and passions. Their message, strong and clear, is "we're old but we're not dead yet."

B.F. Skinner, the noted behavioral psychologist who died at 86 in 1990, was an advocate in his later years of erotic literature and films (porno?) for older people. "It keeps them stimulated and sexually active." This may be controversial but it's probably worth a look.

And fantasizing. We all do it, n'est-ce pas? Even Jimmy Carter, before he was President, said he almost daily lusted after women. And then he went home and prayed to God for forgiveness. In his book, "The Virtues of Aging," President Carter says, "A healthy man who has self-confidence and an accommodating mate can enjoy satisfying and imaginative love play throughout his life." The key words here are "self-confidence" and "accommodating mate."

Our children — Nancy and I have six — are very thoughtful and for our 45th wedding anniversary gave us an outdoor hot tub. Aside from its relaxation of our muscles, it also acts as an aphrodisiac. And believe me, a drug-free aphrodisiac at our age is very nice to have.

I have found there are several advantages of S.O.S. (sex over 60):

1. The curing of the vexing problem of p.e.[1] However, it sometimes slips into p.p.e.[2]

2. ———

Oh, well, my memory isn't too hot either.

And my favorite quote, "Everything takes a little longer but it's time well spent."

1999

---

[1] premature ejaculation

[2] postponed ejaculation

CHAPTER 50

STONE & STENT

The nurse, we'll call her Rea, said, "Take everything off below your waist and lie face up on the stretcher."

I had been planning to go on a trip when a painful kidney stone attacked. Doctor Lou said, "Let's stent it so it doesn't bother you for a while and you can go." I spent a night in the hospital, was anesthetized and an 18-inch stent was inserted into my urinary tract so the stone couldn't move.

Six weeks later, with much stent agitation, a death in the family and no trip, it was time to remove the damned stent. The removal was done in the doctor's office. I was looking forward to getting rid of the stent but not the removal. The thought of having it yanked out in an office procedure sent chills down my spine.

Having followed the nurse's order to strip and lie down, Rea began to sanitize my most private part and then insert some novocaine. I looked up at her and said, "You look familiar. How do I know you?" Rea said, "I used to work for you in your store."

She was an attractive, early middle-aged brunette and I did remember her. Without thinking, I said, "Is this job more interesting?" She turned slightly pink and replied, "I enjoyed working at your store."

Doctor Lou finally came in. They inserted a flexible wire to try and retrieve the stent.

> Doctor - "I think we've got it."
> Nurse - "Not quite — almost."
> Doctor - "There — grab it."
> Nurse - "Oops — just missed."

Finally, the doctor pulled it out. He held up this skinny, slimy-looking tube and said, "This is your stent." My only reply was, "You can keep it!"

As Nurse Rea left to wash up for her next retrieval, she looked me in the eye. "I enjoyed seeing you again."

1999

CHAPTER 51

A FLOWERING POOCH AND COWS

Jeff Koons is an American artist noted for, among other things, marrying *La Cicciolina*, an Italian porn star, and producing erotic art. In my local public library they hide the books on his art. In the Museum of Modern Art in New York, they have neither his art nor his books. However, art collectors like his work. Koons' sculpture of a nude woman in a bathtub sold for $1.7 million at Christie's. He says he has tried to popularize "Bad Taste" and "In part, I'm a con man and a sham."

I've not been a fan of his art. However, when I saw his latest sculpture, I was amazed, amused and delighted. It is a 43-foot high "puppy" sitting where the Christmas tree usually sits in Rockefeller Center.

The "Puppy," as Koons calls it, is covered with soil that is planted with live, growing flowers, over sixty thousand of them—begonias, impatiens, petunias, marigolds, and lobelias. It is in the shape of a West Highland terrier, and it stopped me dead in my tracks and made me smile, say "Wow," and whip out my camera. Not many (any?) sculptures can do that.

The "Puppy" has a stainless steel frame and is watered from the inside. It will change as the flowers grow and the blossoms get bigger. It was first erected in Germany and then Sydney, Australia, and Bilbao, Spain. Now the citizens and tourists of New York have the good fortune to see this attractive, growing, giant creation. It is worth the time and effort to encounter this delightful mammoth young pooch.

Jeff Koons, ever the promoter of his art, says, "The 'Puppy' communicates love, warmth and happiness to everyone." I don't know about love and warmth but it does make me feel happy.

To quote Peter Schjeldahl, the art critic of "The New Yorker," on the "Puppy": "What, exactly, prevents other art from being this good?"

And what else is on the streets of New York these days? Would you believe five hundred life-size fiberglass cows—each painted distinctively by a different artist. This too is happy art.

I saw about ten of these colorful cows in recent trips to New York. The artists whose cows I recognized were Red Grooms' bright red, "Four Alarm Fire Cow" on the street across from the Museum of Modern Art, and LeRoy Nieman's purple, yellow and red cow in the outdoor garden restaurant at Tavern on the Green. At Lincoln Center there are several cows—Moozart, an animal with a dandy's red jacket and a quill in its hoof; and Moodame Butterfly, a black and white cow with a red body covered with butterflies.

Children climb all over these cows to get a "ride" and their parents snap away with their Instamatics. It is not great art but is great fun.

At the end of the summer, the City will auction off all the cows for the benefit of the Parks Department. I wouldn't mind having one for my backyard. However, I feel I will be talked out of it by auction time. My spouse, Nancy, is not a painted-cow fancier, but we'd both love a flowering pooch.

Yes, it was a good summer for outdoor art in exciting New York City, 2000.

2000

CHAPTER 52

VERSACE

Nineteen-ninety-seven was the year of the deaths of the decade — Lady Diana was killed in an auto accident in Paris, her hired driver DUI. And Mother Teresa, icon of Christian caring, died in Bombay.

Most people remember the shooting of Gianni Versace, noted Italian fashion designer, gunned down in front of his home in Miami's South Beach. The assailant was alleged serial killer Andrew Cunanen.

Closer to home, five of my male friends died — cancer (2), heart problems (2) and a suicide. Finally, 1997 ended.

The Metropolitan Museum of Art put on a posthumous exhibition of Versace's fashions in its Costume Institute. I remembered an exquisite presentation there a number of years ago of Yves St. Laurent's work.

Gianni Versace ("Johnny Versochy") was known as a down-to-earth person, but his creations were explosively colorful, flamboyant and very sexy.

I visited the Versace exhibit several times. My first reaction was vulgar, vulgar, vulgar. I expected to see exciting and fashionable, but wearable, ready-to-wear. Nothing I saw would have been worn by anyone I knew. (Though I might have liked to see some of my friends in a few of the outfits.)

My fashion-minded friends could not believe my reaction. They liked what they had seen of Versace, and they knew I always enjoyed lots of color, liveliness and flamboyance. So I decided to return to the Met for a second look.

I took it more slowly. I read the explanatory cards by each outfit, and I bought and enjoyed the gorgeously illustrated book about the exhibit published by the Met.

I learned that Versace was an earthy, reflective man who read and re-read Proust. He looked to the street for his inspiration and styling, and chose the prostitute as his fashion ideal. To quote from the exhibit book by Costume Curator Richard Martin:

> His valorization of the prostitute was an exquisite choice, recognizing the independence and strength of the street-walker, not as an enslaved sex worker but as an autonomous, self-defining figure of awesome visual authority among the ambiguous and compromised figures of modern visual culture.

I couldn't have said it better myself.

Versace's glorification of sex in fashion was not merely as a fact of life — but as a "celebration of life." He designed for the "strong sensuous woman of unabashed sexuality."

One of his most famous creations shown in the exhibit was the Elizabeth Hurley dress. It was a long, black silk evening gown with silver and gold safety pins as ornamentation. The dress was slit at the sides and six-inch safety pins went down the gown, leaving about four inches of skin exposed. "Versace rendered the little black dress more revealing and more voluptuous than ever." An eye-popper.

Another outfit that caught my attention was a dress with a tantalizing short skirt and a vivacious 18th Century print of flowers and dancers. The low V-neckline was revealing and the shoulders were covered with a blue denim jacket with gold buttons and jewelry. Startling but fun.

Versace used unusual fabrics to make his fashion statement. A short dress with cut-out midriff and gold buttons was made of a shiny, bright yellow vinyl. And he did a similar midriff-baring number in hot pink vinyl. An even more eye-catching dress was a short, see-through vinyl one edged in red beading with a scattering of rhinestones and gold beaded flowers. Most intriguing.

Gianni V. was influenced by contemporary artists such as Calder, Lichtenstein, Dine and Warhol. His Warhol dress was highly colored — red, yellow, blue, green, and orchid — a very slinky long dress in the Warhol images of Marilyn Monroe and James Dean. On the breast was a swirl of multi-colored ribbons with the ribbons extending over bare shoulders. Monroe, Dean and Warhol were dead when this was designed, but the dress really came alive. His Lichtenstein dress was a yellow, see-through "wham" outfit with bright yellow panties.

All these dresses were shown on white plastic mannequins and, yes, I would like to see them on friends and acquaintances.

About 10% of Versace's work was designed for men. His designs were for men as sex objects — lusty males with gym-built upper torsos. To show off the male form, his shirts and jackets were loose and his slacks and jeans tight. Color was mostly black with a smattering of wild prints such as the bright Warhol print featured in his women's wear. I'm not a fan of black and don't have a gym-built torso, so I wasn't taken with his men's fashions.

However, his women's wear had excitement and sex appeal, so my verdict the second time around was - fun, fun, fun!

1997

CHAPTER 53

THE WORLDS

One hundred of the world's best sunfish sailors were given brand-new sailboats — all with colorful red and blue sails — to race in the 1998 World's Championship off Blue Point, Long Island. Our club, The Sayville Yacht Club, was the host and sailors from ten different countries entered.

It was an exciting and colorful event. To see 100 bright red and blue sails all lined up in a row awaiting the starting gun was a truly memorable sight. They looked like a large flock of blue-tailed cardinals on a long telephone wire. Then came the surge at the gun with the top-rated sailors always seeming to jump into the lead.

There were eight races during the week — two a day. The weather varied from moderately calm to the threat of a hurricane on the final day. I was on a patrol boat for two of the days and as a photographer got a major charge out of the racing scene and some pretty good pictures, too. It was especially thrilling to see six or eight of these red and blue fish go around the orange markers all at one time, each trying for the advantage, and not crashing into their close-by competitors. On the final day, with a heavy chop from an impending storm, nine or ten boats flipped over with some of the finest sailors.

The racers were all sizes and ages from 15 to the 70's. One petite young woman Nancy H. (under 100 pounds) won a race in calm waters and was ecstatic about her victory. "I won! I won! I can sail with the best of them!"

Another racer was a completely bald young man from South Carolina who had a serious cancer problem but chose to forego his chemotherapy for a week so he could compete. He sailed for three races, beating 70 boats in one, but his strength left him and he watched the last five races. "But it was a wonderful week and I'm looking forward to racing again," he said as he left for home.

I met Ann and Marty MacColgain from Dublin, Ireland. Marty was a linguist who was strongly into his Gaelic heritage — thus his two teenage sons who were in the races were named Siaghal and Diarmaid. Siaghal did well — finishing in the top half. Diarmaid dropped out after three races due to a shoulder injury. However, the Dubliners did seem to relish their Long Island experience.

Our yacht club had several entrants in the competition. One, Kathy, an attractive young lady with two children, is a restaurant manager. She is in line to be our Commodore next year and is a very competent sailor. She beat out 58 other sailors.

A local racer, Paul-Jon, from Blue Point finished near the top in every race but one (the calm day) and made a valiant effort to be the '98 world champion.

One of the sailors, Dave, a physics professor from upstate New York, stayed with us and entertained us with his delicious sense of humor. He had been the North American champion at one time but, since he was close to 60 and not in the greatest shape, he struggled against many of the younger competitors. He talked about his need for "more vitamins and Viagra" and said it would take him two weeks to recover from the eight races. We were sure he would be racing again the next weekend.

The final day I was patrolling with a friend and two young women from Mississippi. They were delightful and funny and insisted on calling us "SIR." Their husbands were competing and doing well, 5th and 12th. Between races we dashed over to Fire Island to secure my friend's house from hurricane Bonnie—which never really arrived. Our southern passengers had never seen Fire Island or such an angry Atlantic Ocean and seemed to thrive on this diversion.

Back at the last races drama for the lead was building. The favorite, Malcom S. from Bermuda, was in a very close race with our own P.J. for the championship. Toward the finish of the 7th race in very choppy, hurricane fringed waters P.J.'s rudder broke. He finished but lost time and his boat was disabled. He appealed to the race judges and was given 2nd which was where he was when disabled. Malcom ended up with one less point (lowest score wins) 23 to 24, and thus became the 1998 World Sunfish Champion.

At the award's banquet Malcom was gracious, "P.J. and I will be battling it out for supremacy for years to come."

P.J. said it was a good race week and he was, of course, disappointed but his future looked bright as he was getting married in the fall.

It was a great week for The Sayville Yacht Club and for sailing.

1998

CHAPTER 54

OUR MONASTERY

I am a Protestant, but some of my most memorable spiritual experiences have been in Roman Catholic settings — a Trappist monastery in Colorado for example.

I've been fortunate to go skiing in Colorado with family and friends. Because of ageing bones and muscles, I ski every other day; on the non-ski days I enjoy driving around the back country of the Aspen-Snowmass area.

One day in the back hills around Old Snowmass, I came across a sign that read: "St. Benedict's Monastery." I'd never been to a monastery, so I decided to follow the arrow. First I passed a farm house and a barn with several farm animals. I continued to follow the snow covered road until I saw, nestled in the valley below snow-capped mountains, a rambling khaki green building with peaked roofs. In the center is a handsome bell tower topped by a steeple and golden cross. It looked like a scene out of "The Sound of Music." Soon another sign said: "Please Do Not Go Any Further." I stopped, took a picture of this idyllic setting and drove off.

That evening I mentioned the monastery to Bonnie, a skiing friend. She said, "You know what? My uncle Paul is a priest who came to Colorado to start a monastic retreat." We wondered...

The next day or so I drove with Bonnie and my wife, Nancy, back to the monastery in that remote valley miles from nearest neighbors. We stopped at the "No Further" sign and noticed a car coming toward us from the building in the valley. An older priest was in the car and he stopped to talk to us. Bonnie asked if he knew her uncle, Father Paul Shiebler. He replied, "Yes — he and I started this monastery 20 years ago." The driver was Father Thomas Keating, a noted Catholic theologian and resident of St. Benedict's. He told us that the monks have morning worship services at 7:30 and that we were welcome. Since then we have gone to services in the chapel several dozen times.

The chapel is a long, high-ceilinged room with benches around the sides and back for lay visitors and chairs arranged in an oval in the center for the white-cowled monks, usually about a dozen. Sometimes the monk giving the homily is dressed in a purple or dark colored robe.

The chapel's floor is burnt orange brick and the ceiling is tawny, honey colored wood. The walls are rose weathered brick. At the far end is a table covered with a purple cloth upon which are a Bible, a candle and a cup and plate for communion. A thin wrought iron cross on a stand with the crucified Jesus upon it is next to the table. On the farthest wall is a tall, narrow, stained glass window of the Madonna and Child. And on each side there are windows looking out towards the mountains. There is an overwhelming feeling of serenity and contemplativeness in this simple but lovely chapel with these dedicated men of the cloth.

Much of the service is sung — in English — and the blending of the male voices is like a resonating, low-pitched bell. Two of the monks have especially fine voices and are given the solo parts. The Bible is read, a homily is given, usually by a senior monk and then prayers are offered, often by several monks about friends who are ill or other personal concerns. After this we all, the monks and the lay guests, stand in a circle and receive communion, given by two of the monks. It is, as they go around the circle proffering the bread and the wine to each of us, a very spiritual time in the service.

The most interesting aspect of our visits to St. Benedict's is seeing the monks in their monastic setting and getting to know several of them. Usually there are twelve monks at the worship service — all sizes, shapes and ages. One was an angular 6'7" and next to him sat a short 5'0" monk who wore a wool skull cap. One time we saw a handsome, young, red-headed monk (novice). My young daughters, 24, 26 and 27, were especially anxious to meet him and we got to chat with him after the service. He told us he had been a California surfer and had gotten into drugs and then decided to enter the monastic life. We never saw him again.

Father William Meninger is a round faced, white haired, chubby monk who has written extensively about the monastic life. In his book, "1012 Monastery Road," he writes:

> For some the words "monastic" and "contemplative" are almost synonymous. To be a monk is to be a contemplative, to witness to the value of contemplation and to share this value with those who resonate to it and wish to support and strengthen it in themselves. This sharing is indeed a viable part of monastic spirituality, and is the reason why we Trappist monks write books and even occasionally leave our monasteries to give conferences, workshops, and retreats. But above all, our witness is in the living, in the abiding communal expression of the contemplative attitude.

At St. Benedict's, the monastic witness to contemplation occurs in an hour-long period of meditation at 4:00 a.m. daily. At 6:00 p.m. there is another hour of meditation.

The Abbot of St. Benedict's is Father Joseph, a fine looking, well-spoken man who exudes warmth and functions as the CEO.

After the worship service, we are able to talk to some of the monks in the library/sales parlor adjacent to the chapel. To support themselves they bake and sell cookies, delicious by the way, and also farm the land. They also conduct intensive week-long retreats for lay people in a new building one-half mile away, built especially for that purpose.

In the library where the monks sell their cookies, there are also crucifixes, mementos of the monastery, and quite a variety of books, including books on sex, women's issues and animals. "Violence Against Women and Children," "Medieval Women Monastics—Wisdom Wellspring," "Sex is Holy," and "God's Dogs—North American Coyotes" are some of the titles, plus a number of books and tapes authored by some of the monks in residence, Fathers Keating, Meninger and Theophane.

Father Theophane is the monk we've gotten to know the best over the years. He is a tall, gaunt, tousle-haired man with a slow, stooped gait. He has a wonderful twinkle in his eyes and a friendly, pixieish sense of humor. He greets us with, "What brought you people slumming?" I remember a homily he gave about the sister of St. Benedict, her wonderful virtues and the importance of women in the Church. This was at a service when four nuns from Iowa were visiting. He told me later, "There was a lot of tension in the air when the nuns were here." What kind of tension was left to the imagination.

Father Theophane speaks fondly of his twin sister who was at one time the mayor of Mineola, Long Island, and still serves that community. He mentioned the tragedies in her life — the death of a five-year-old son and then a miscarriage. He said, "She then decided to go out — not in — and got involved in community and parish activities, including local politics." He recently visited his sister on Long Island, when she was feted as "Citizen of the Year."

Theophane is ecumenical and progressive. He has traveled widely, including India, has become familiar with Buddhism and has met the Dalai Lama. He is friends with other clergy in the Aspen-Snowmass area and has conferred with the Jewish philosopher Mortimer Adler, who summers in Aspen.

He spoke of the growth of Buddhism and Eastern religions in America and the stagnation of the Catholic Church — especially in attracting young men into the priesthood and monkhood.

Theophane seems to enjoy chatting with our family. Three of our daughters are devotees of the Siddha Yoga Guru Gurumayi; Nancy and I are liberal Congregationalists. He appears quite impressed with Nancy, mother of six. And his first question to me the last time I saw him was, "What are you daughters up to these days?"

Theophane the Roman Catholic monk appears to like to shock us with his negative views on the present Pope and the Vatican. I asked him what he thought were the chances for the ordination of women in the Catholic Church. He said he had recently read that the same question had been asked of Cardinal Martini of Milan, a potential candidate for the next Pope. The cardinal's answer was, "Not in this century." Our monk friend was encouraged to believe that after 2000 things might change.

I told Theophane that we had a gay minister in our hometown church. What did he think about the acceptance of gay people? "It's coming." He told the story of the woman who said to him, "Everyone in India is a sinner. They don't believe in Jesus." He replied, at least to me, "God made us all as individuals and gave us the brains to <u>think</u> not just follow dogma by rote."

He has written a charming book called "Tales of a Magic Monastery." In it he tells stories to illustrate his views. For example:

> Why did I visit the Magic Monastery? Well, I'm a monk myself, and the strangest thing happened in my monastery. We had a visit from the Buddha. We prepared for it, and gave him a very warm, though solemn welcome. He stayed overnight, but he slipped away very early in the morning. When the monks woke up, they found graffiti all over the cloister walls. Imagine! One word: TRIVIA, TRIVIA, TRIVIA, all over the place.

I guess "Love Thy Neighbor" says it all.

All of our visits to St. Benedict's Monastery have meant a great deal to our family — educationally, spiritually and culturally. Once we went to the chapel on Ash Wednesday. This was a first for all of us. It was a very simple ceremony. Father Keating put ashes on each of our foreheads and we all felt proud and humbled by this Christian symbol on our faces.

The spiritual bonding between Nancy and me and our Guru-embracing daughters adds a wonderful extra dimension to our monastery visits.

1998

CHAPTER 55

GAYS IN THE PULPIT

For 26 years we had a modern-day prophet for a minister in our church, the Sayville United Church of Christ on the south shore of Long Island. Trevor Hausske, our minister, was a person who lived his Christian preaching 24 hours a day, 7 days a week. He was not a dynamic preacher and was rather a quiet, unostentatious individual. But he never failed to reach out and help someone whoever that person might be — in or out of our church — night or day. He also was a strong civil rights activist and risked his life by going to Selma, Alabama for that infamous march. When the civil rights questions cooled down Trevor became an advocate for women's rights and for inclusive language.

When Hausske retired a pastoral search committee was formed to find a successor and I was fortunate enough to be on it. We reviewed over 70 applications, listened to numerous tapes, made countless telephone calls and met almost weekly for an entire year.

The committee was a diverse group — liberal and moderate, young and retired — and we had lively discussions on religious directions, social concerns, interpretations of the Bible, intellectualism and fundamentalism. It was one of the most stimulating things I've ever done.

We had surveys in our church and called meetings to determine what the congregation was looking for — a strong preacher, good with the young people, a sensitive counselor, good on visitations, etc. etc.

There was one applicant we kept coming back to — John Geter. He was a recent Yale Divinity School graduate but had not been ordained. His application was very thoughtful, a notch above most of the others; his recommendations were absolutely outstanding. "Dynamic preacher," "Wonder with all ages," "The best at Yale in quite some time," "Destined to be an important minister in the U.C.C."

He had worked in churches in the New Haven area, had previously been an off-Broadway actor and director and had been active in AIDS-related social work. We talked to his mentors at Yale and received nothing but the highest commendations.

Finally we brought him to Sayville for an interview and to listen to him preach. He was a smallish fair-haired man who looked younger than his 31 years. We were very pleased with him. We speculated about his sexuality but did not at first ask him. The chairperson of our search committee, Caroline, was an open lesbian.

At that point I left on a three-week vacation. In the meantime John revealed to the committee that he was gay. It was decided not to announce this to our congregation at the time. He told us that if he were voted in, he would stay at least five years and he would let the congregation know of his sexuality in six months to a year.

He was presented to the church and was voted in unanimously. Several months later he was ordained in a church in New Haven. The program for his ordination said that he was dedicating the service to his "companion for life — Bob." The program had been printed by a member in our church and the word was out! It didn't take long for strong opposition to form. "Why didn't the committee tell us?" "I have nothing against gays but not for my spiritual leaders." "We have been misled and mistreated."

My own position on gay people was tolerance with a tinge of wariness. I worked with homosexuals in my business — some in executive positions, had gay relatives in my extended family and knew several close friends whose children had recently "come out." I was sympathetic to their plight in America.

Our now divided church had meetings and counseling sessions and many rather heated discussions. Finally it was decided to have an open church meeting where both sides — for and against John — could make brief comments.

A vote was taken and John was asked to stay on by a two to one margin. This, of course, didn't end the problem. Those who voted against retaining John had to make their personal decisions about remaining or leaving the church. Most decided to leave, and we lost almost one-third of our membership. However, those who stayed were supportive of John and determined to keep our church going. We did gain some new members — mostly gay people — and continued to maintain our financial and social viability.

John was a very bright, articulate and compassionate, and engendered much love and support in our church. He did change "companions for life" but no one said much.

After two years he and our church leadership decided to vote on becoming "an open and affirming church" — meaning we were open to all people regardless of sexual orientation. There was some opposition. I, myself, felt we were as open and affirming as a church could be and didn't need to stir up more emotions on this issue since there were still families opposed. However, I did not vote against this and it won with 90% support.

Just shy of three years into his ministry John announced he had been offered a fellowship for further study at Yale and felt he could not turn it down. Many of us were disappointed but we all wished him well and he returned to New Haven.

Another search committee was formed with a new group of members. They looked at over 100 applications and finally decided on Diane Darling of California. The letter announcing our decision also mentioned she was coming with her partner, Elaine. My reaction — and that of many others — was, "Oh, shit!"

Diane certainly appeared to be an outstanding candidate. She even said in her first sermon, "I'm sure many of you are saying, 'not again!'"

Diane made a good first impression but within a matter of weeks she had a major back problem and had back surgery, requiring several months healing, so she got off to a slow start. One or two people left the church (not everyone was thrilled with having a woman minister — let alone a lesbian).

When she returned to the church, Diane was quite a good preacher, and soon we had taken in 18 new members, 17 women including a fair share of lesbians.

We have a strong, loving, outreaching church now and I feel good about the present situation. It is certainly heart-warming to know that openly gay and lesbian people have a church they can go to and feel comfortable and wanted. They are a strong part of our church and wonderful Christians.

None of us, straight or gay, want a mostly gay church. Thus the challenge facing Diane and all of us is how to attract heterosexual couples (hopefully with children, as our Sunday school has diminished in size) into our church to keep an even balance.

My association in our church with gay ministers and parishioners has certainly extended my tolerance for their sexuality and increased my awareness of the homophobia that they face every day. I can see that much of homosexual love appears to be at least as strong and binding as what often passes today for heterosexual love.

Recently our church received a letter from Reverend John Geter telling us that he had been HIV positive since before he came to our church as our minister. He ended his letter saying, "Finally I want you to pray and hope for me, for my embodied spirit and for my still-spirited body, that I may continue to know God's love and care during this difficult time. I will offer the same prayer for you. With many, many thanks and much love, John."

Postscripts

Three and a half years after leaving our church, John Geter died of AIDS.

Diane Darling and her partner split after two years with our church. A year later Diane left us to return to the West Coast.

Ten years later I am on another pastoral search committee. We are determined to get the best possible minister regardless of sexual orientation.

1999

CHAPTER 56

FATHER KELLY IN AFRICA

I met Joseph Kelly before he was a priest. We worked together in my grandfather's department store. He was quiet, soft-spoken and conscientious, and fifty years later he is still square-jawed and open-faced with a warm smile.

When Joseph was growing up his best friend and neighbor was a lonely African-American. Joseph saw the problems faced by African-Americans and decided he wanted to help his black friend's people. Joseph studied with the Holy Ghost Fathers and, in 1950, was ordained a Catholic priest and sent to Tanzania in East Africa as a missionary. His first assignment was a mission station on the slopes of Mt. Kilimanjaro, and he later said Mass in the snow atop that volcanic mountain.

Father Kelly came back to the United States every two years for R & R and stopped in at our family store. We ate up his stories of living and working in the African bush. We gave him shirts and a lightweight suit, and he sent us a letter of thanks along with yearly Christmas greetings from Africa.

One year, when Father Kelly was back in Tanzania, he wrote to us his church needed carpeting. We picked out what we thought was appropriate - a kind of indoor/outdoor carpet for a humid climate - and sent it to a diocese in Wisconsin to be forwarded to Africa.

A year or so later, my wife and I, along with four friends, joined a Dartmouth College tour to East Africa. At one point, we found ourselves in Arusha, Tanzania, not far from Father Kelly's mission in Usa River. How exciting it would be to visit Father Kelly's outpost! He was only four or five miles away, so I tried to call him. After forty-five minutes of delays, interruptions and cut-offs, I got hold of him. He said he'd drive his truck over and take us to his village. After a very bumpy ride in the back of his pick-up - all the roads in Tanzania are badly rutted - we arrived in a small village with a church and numerous buildings stretched out on a dusty road along the river.

The church is a large cement block building with hand-made stained glass windows and wooden benches for 750 people. Father Kelly said several times a year it was wall-to-wall parishioners. Father Kelly pointed out the carpet from our store. As we entered, we noticed a young altar boy pouring water into a sacramental urn. He looked up with big, round, amazed eyes to see seven white faces coming toward him. At that point, the water spilled all over the carpet.

At the back of the church was a wooden container labeled "Poor Box." Father Kelly said, "There is always someone in greater need than the people in our parish."

We walked around the village and met several colorfully dressed women balancing sacks of grain on their heads. They smiled broadly as they saw Father Kelly, and he introduced us to them, in Swahili, as "friends from my village back home." We also met Father John, an African priest who had been trained by Father Kelly. He was a tall, fine-looking man with an endearing smile, and wore a long, white shirt. Father John was soon to become the priest for a tribe of Masai twenty miles away.

We than passed a small open-fronted building with a corrugated steel roof and two cots inside. Out front, the sign said "Guest House." Another building was the village store, where an old woman squatted on her haunches, selling food and utensils - beans, bananas, coconuts, baskets, etc. I bought a straw whisk broom, which I have cherished ever since. The houses on the street were neat, clean and sparse, with dirt floors, wooden beds and small cooking areas.

Further down the street was a small dispensary used by a visiting nurse once or twice a week to treat, as best she could, malaria, eye problems and the growing scourge of AIDS.

We saw several children running gaily about and were particularly attracted to the boys, about eight-years-old, who were playing in the dirt with hand-made wire and tin-can toys. We blew up some balloons we had brought and gave them to the boys. Nothing could have pleased them more, except perhaps the pieces of candy we also handed over. I took a memorable picture of these youngsters with their crude toys, holding the bright new balloons and chewing on some sweets.

Father Kelly demonstrated the village's ultimate recycling system to obtain cooking and lantern fuel. The villagers grew corn to make corn flour. The waste from the corn was fed to the pigs. The waste from the pigs was put in a pit where it emitted a methane gas. The gas was piped into the kitchen area and used for light and fire for the stove. We were served a delicious hot breakfast of tea and scrambled eggs cooked by this methane gas. Nothing in Africa tasted better.

On our African safari we were intrigued by the many wild animals we saw. We were lucky(?) enough to see two lions stalk and kill a zebra and saw hippos cavorting in water holes with crocodiles languishing on the nearby shore. But nothing touched us and interested us as much as having Father Kelly proudly show us the human scene in the African bush. People are always the most fascinating part of any trip.

Father Kelly is pleased that, under the leadership of Roman Catholic Julius Nyere and his successors, Tanzania has progressed without violence or civil war. I recently asked him how the United States looks from Africa. He said we are a rich, progressive and helpful country, but we could be more helpful and that we sometimes embarrass him. "How?" "The antics of Ollie North and Clinton and your immature, childlike Congress — especially the way they went after Clinton."

This year, 2000, Father Kelly celebrates his 75th birthday and fifty years as a missionary in Africa. He obviously loves Africa and its people and is fulfilled and happy with his life of service to God and to that impoverished continent.

2000

CHAPTER 57

TREVOR

Trevor Hausske was born in China about seventy years ago. His father was a missionary administrator in the Chinese-American Hospital near Peking. Trevor lived in China his first 18 years, then came to America and became a high school science teacher. Later he attended Yale Divinity School and served churches in Wisconsin, Connecticut and, finally, in Sayville, New York, where he was our minister for 26 years.

After he retired, he and his wonderful wife Marjean traveled with Nancy and me to China. What a treat to go to China with someone who had lived there fifty years ago and spoke the language fluently. Trevor is tall, handsome and white-haired. The Chinese people he met were fascinated by this exotic American who spoke their language.

In Chungking, Trevor and I walked into a residential apartment area. He was soon surrounded by a crowd of Chinese smiling and asking numerous questions: "How old are you and your friend?" "What do you do?" "How come you speak so well?" "Do you like China?"

Another time we were in a small park in Wuhan on the Yangste River. Several Chinese senior citizens were sitting around chatting, and on a small stage, an elderly man was singing, accompanied by two musicians playing ancient stringed instruments. Trevor spoke with the singer and discovered that he had sung with the Beijing Opera Company. Soon they, Trevor and the opera singer, were encouraged to sing a duet from a Chinese song they both knew. It was a touching moment for all of us. They received a warm reception and bowed formally to each other.

Twenty-six years is a very long time for a minister to serve one church. Trevor is much loved by the people of our Sayville UCC Church and he leaves a lasting and important gift.

Trevor's legacy is the life that he leads. I have never met a more selfless, caring person. Any time, day or night, he was willing, even anxious, to help whomever he could, whoever needed help, whether a parishioner or not. Some of the latest scholarship on the life of Jesus claims that there is little historical basis for many of the words attributed to Him. However, the point made is that His life is what is important and has had such a worldwide impact for 2,000 years. Trevor has dedicated his life to spreading the Word of God, and his caring life has a strong impact on our family and community.

What I remember from his sermons is the word "forgiveness." When I mentioned this to him recently, he said that forgiveness was one of a number of ideas he had tried to get across. It is something that has certainly helped me and has become a cornerstone of my religious beliefs.

He brought two remarkable women to our area. His first wife, Dorothy Lee Davidson Hauske, our choir director and a high school music teacher, was one of the most brilliant and talented women I've ever known. Strong-minded, outspoken, and unsettled in her role as a minister's wife, she was one of the first vociferous women's rights women I met. She wrote a rock musical, "Emmanuel," which I consider one of the most exciting theater pieces I've seen. It was produced off-Broadway and in many UCC churches with amateur musicians, singers and dancers. It has lovely 20th century hymns and, I hope someday it will receive the national recognition it deserves. The message of "Emmanuel" is "I care — I am with you."

As time went on, Dorothy Lee became more and more difficult. She was diagnosed with a brain tumor from which she died. Trevor mourned her for almost two years. Then one day he was introduced to a minister's widow from Minnesota. They dated and finally married, and Marjean Postlethwaite was brought into our community as our Trevor's new wife. Like Dorothy Lee, she was a musician and became our choir director. Marjean reminds me of Eleanor Roosevelt — not glamorous but relaxed and yet exciting and fun to be around. She continues to make Trevor's retired life happy.

While he was our minister, Trevor put his life on the line for his beliefs. He passionately believed in civil rights and went to Canton, Mississippi, to march and stand up for his convictions during the period of civil strife in the South. He was shadowed by rednecks with shotguns in pickups while his wife received calls back in Sayville threatening his life. He now believes he and his fellow protestors were the original targets when Chaney and Goodman were killed. He returned safely but not without several close calls.

Several years after Trevor retired, his strong stand for civil rights and women's rights set the stage for our church to receive the Burning Bush Award for our efforts for gay and lesbian rights. Trevor's successor was a wonderful young man from Yale Divinity School, who was gay. Sadly, Trevor's only son was gay and died of AIDS.

Trevor appears to be a mild-mannered person with a fairly even temperament, but he has a steely character and he is a terror on the tennis court. I am fortunate in being able to call him one of my very best friends. He is a model of Christian perseverance and humility.

1998

CHAPTER 58

EMMANUEL

My favorite musicals on the stage are "My Fair Lady," "South Pacific," "Kiss Me Kate" and recently "Contact." But none give me the joy, the pleasure, the emotional jolt of "Emmanuel." It is the soul-satisfying essence of Christmas told with beautiful and original music and lyrics. "Emmanuel" is a folk, blues, good news musical written by Dorothy Davidson Hausske. It was written in 1972 for our Sayville Congregational Church as a Christmas musical and was an instant hit. It has been performed in Maine, Massachusetts, Rochester, New York and off-Broadway.

Our church revives it every five years or so and it gets better every time. It is performed, mostly, by amateur musicians and dancers from local churches, but the results to me are professional and overwhelming. I've seen it about fifteen times and get a bigger delight out of it each time I watch it.

The author, everyone called her Dorothy Lee, was the wife of Trevor Hausske, our minister for 26 years. She didn't relish playing the role of a minister's wife but became our choir director (minister of music). She did a bang-up job, bringing life and passion and musical excitement to our church services. I have never known a more intelligent and sharp-minded person. Dorothy Lee was an early and committed advocate for women's rights, and for helping the plight of the farmer-laborer — remember Cesar Chavez?

Dorothy Lee rode around in a battered old pale-yellow Mercedes sedan, and taught music in school and piano at home. When she was in her late 40's she developed severe headaches. She later died of a brain tumor. But "Emmanuel" lives on and continues to get standing ovations at sold-out performances.

The latest performance, December '99 was as exciting as ever. My own reaction, again, was tears of pleasure and joy throughout the presentation, a reaction shared by many. It's a lively exuberant musical with bright costumes and wonderfully meaningful and tuneful songs.

Dorothy Lee, in her notes on "Emmanuel," quotes the martyred German theologian, Dietrich Bonhoeffer, "We must live in the world as if there is no God; we must take care of each other as though there is no one else to do it." She goes on to write, "Bonhoeffer left the safety of American academic life to be with his people in time of terror. When he resisted Nazi inhumanity they imprisoned him. They killed him, but he was with his people. "Emmanuel" is about the promises we make, and the ultimate one 'I care, I am with you'!"

The musical is sung by a mixed chorus of adults and young children. One song goes — "The questions the children ask are the questions we ask till we die

— where is God? Who is my brother? Who am I?" and the children repeat in song "Who am I?" Mary and Joseph travel to Bethlehem and are rebuffed at the Inn. Jesus is born in a manger in the stable. The chorus sings a lovely song, "There's a star in the east on Christmas morn. Rise up shepherd and follow that star." "Emmanuel" finishes with the lively and stirring "All around the rocking cradle — take my hand.

God with us

Emmanuel

Bethlehem

Room at the Inn

Peace for the Earth

TAKE MY HAND!"

1999

CHAPTER 59

THE REAL JESUS

I have always had a fascination for what history said about the life of Jesus and His teachings. In our church we had an interim minister, Wes Sheffield, who continued to pique my interest in these subjects. In a Bible study class he introduced us to The Five Gospels, a book the Jesus Seminar published about the historical accuracy of the New Testament teachings of Jesus. The Jesus Seminar is a group of Biblical scholars, both liberal and conservative, who decide as a working group whether New Testament passages are: (a) historically based, (b) paraphrased, or (c) simply the words of the Apostles without historical basis. The Five Gospels contends 80% of what was written about Jesus belongs in category b or c.

While visiting Florida, I was fortunate enough to hear a lecture by John Dominic Crossan, one of the authors of The Five Gospels and a noted and quoted Jesus scholar.

Crossan, a former Catholic priest, is now a retired professor of theology. He lectures around the country on his historical beliefs on the life of Jesus. He is a short, thin man, originally from Ireland, with an Irish twinkle and wit, and has a fascinating story to tell. Crossan does not believe that all the sayings attributed to Jesus are accurate. Also he does not believe that "all the good stuff came from Jesus and all the rest is wrong." Much of the teaching of Jesus is wisdom filtered down over the years by His followers. Mark, the earliest Apostle to write about Jesus, did not begin until almost 50 years after Jesus' death.

Crossan believes strongly that it was Jesus' life not His words that was of greatest importance. Leading a life of caring and healing and breaking bread with others is the example that spread to His followers and has continued for 2,000 years. Jesus sent out His followers to heal the sick and eat with the people, as He did, thus spreading His idea of the Kingdom of God.

Crossan has strong feelings about Jesus' death. Historically there is no question He was crucified. The Resurrection is another story. Did the tomb open and Jesus appear again in the flesh? "Probably not." His followers and only His followers may have seen an apparition. Certainly people experienced Jesus after His death, as today millions still do. To Crossan, Resurrection means experiencing Jesus later, and now people are still being healed and cared for.

This is apt to be controversial stuff, especially for conservative Christians. Many of the 250 people at Crossan's lecture stayed for several hours after his 50-minute lecture to question and challenge him. He was, I thought, fair and precise and knowledgeable and thoughtful in his answers. I certainly learned from him and I agree with his basic points.

Oh yes, Heaven. Prof. Crossan says Heaven is beside the point. Get on with working toward the Kingdom of God on earth now. Heaven can wait. <u>Amen</u>!

1999

ACKNOWLEDGEMENT

The Joys and Jolts of Retirement

ACKNOWLEDGEMENT

Special thanks go to my wife Nancy, my children John, Dana, Karen, Barbara, Trish and Carolyn, Joe Medlicott, Barbara Krieger, Terry Osborne, Priscilla Sears, Noel Perrin, Beverly Smith, Valerie Turnbull, Carol Lamb, Deborah Newham, Barbara Mosley and last but not least Suzan Saxon.

149

Printed in the United States
3266